N.A.1

THE NORTH-SOUTH

CONTINENTAL HIGHWAY

LOOKING SOUTH

LOOKING NORTH
LOOKING SOUTH

N.A. 1

THE NORTH-SOUTH
CONTINENTAL HIGHWAY

LOOKING

SOUTH

by George R. Stewart

maps by Erwin Raisz

THE RIVERSIDE PRESS · CAMBRIDGE

HOUGHTON MIFFLIN COMPANY · BOSTON

1957

• Books by George R. Stewart

BRET HARTE

ORDEAL BY HUNGER

JOHN PHOENIX

EAST OF THE GIANTS

DOCTOR'S ORAL

STORM

NAMES ON THE LAND

MAN: AN AUTOBIOGRAPHY

FIRE

EARTH ABIDES

THE YEAR OF THE OATH (in collaboration)

SHEEP ROCK

U.S. 40

AMERICAN WAYS OF LIFE

THE YEARS OF THE CITY

N.A. 1

The Riverside Press
CAMBRIDGE • MASSACHUSETTS

To my companions on the road—

Theodosia, Franklin, Parker, and Hal

CONTENTS

LOOKING SOUTH

LOOKING BOTH WAYS

Looking South

ON DRIVING SOUTH

As to the adventure of driving south — even as to whether it should still be called an adventure — that is a difficult subject on which to write, since things will be certain to change in the necessary lapse of time between writing and publication. The highway in Mexico, to be sure, presents few problems; in 1955 it was all established, and all paved except for fifty well-graveled miles south of San Cristóbal. The best I can do, south of Mexico, is to present driving-conditions as I found them, brought up to date by information received late in 1956. At that time the opening of El Tapón seemed likely for late 1957 . . .

In Central America the highway is about 1100 miles in length. I found about half of it paved. A little of this consisted of what might be called modern paving, that is, a highway constructed according to specifications established for the Pan-American Highway. The rest of the paved section may be compared to the highways that were being built throughout the United States in the twenties. It is of a cramped two-lane width, with inadequate shoulders. In hilly and mountainous districts it winds excessively, and has fairly steep grades. The grades do not bother one of our power-happy American giants, but the narrowness and twistiness make a driver long for one of the agile little European cars, or for one of our small models of the thirties. Still, there is nothing dangerous about such a road if it is driven carefully, and the swinging curves often open up unexpected vistas.

In 1955 the unpaved half of the highway could be classed as "all-weather gravel," though a few stretches hardly came up to that level, and I should not have liked to drive them in a heavy rain. But these were short, and were marked for improvement. This improvement, by the way, is something that you will not actually welcome when you come upon it in progress, because it means that sections of the road are torn up and in bad shape.

The PRA engineers have orders to keep the passage practical for cars at all times; where Mexican or Central American road-crews are at work, they are not always so careful.

Many of the photographs demonstrate, better than verbal descriptions can do, the actual condition of the highway in 1955.

Before long — once it has been put through according to PRA standards — the Pan-American Highway is going to be one of the most delightful roads in the world, merely to drive. So much can be said for it already in Mexico.

I am not now referring primarily to what may be seen from it, but am thinking of the driver's own pleasure. It will not be like one of our great turnpikes or freeways — multiple-laned, with curves so easy as to be imperceptible, almost brutally imposed upon the face of the countryside by the cutting down of hills and the filling up of valleys. On such a road the driver almost loses the sense of having a powerful car as a kind of extension of his own body, and the driver and his passengers alike lose the sense of a countryside, because it has literally been steam-rollered away.

I recognize only three uses of such a turnpike or freeway. It enables me to get somewhere quickly if I am in a hurry; it lets me move easily through long and dreary outskirts of our cities; it channels off most of the traffic, so that I can drive the second-string highways with some degree of pleasure.

Neither in Mexico nor in Central America is the southern road one of these modern monstrosities, and it will not be for a long time. As the pictures show, it still keeps going over and around hills, not cutting through or tunneling under them. If it winds through a canyon, you still know that a canyon is there. It does not by-pass all the villages and towns, and so you see what they are like. And, all the time, you know you are really driving a car and feel the pleasant sense of achievement that goes with that knowledge.

You are safer driving south of the border than driving the same distance on one of our highways in the United States, because you are not exposed to the dangers of heavy traffic. There are, indeed, certain special hazards. They should be discussed, partly because the automobilist should take precautions against them, and partly because they arise from some interesting habits of the countries traversed.

First of all, naturally, one should take precaution by realizing that ordinary insurance is not valid in the southern countries and by taking out a proper policy. Such a policy is useful not only for financial protection but also because it gives you the local agent as a person to be on your side in case of trouble.

As for the special hazards of driving, they can be discussed under only two heads — the road, and things on it.

The former have been partially presented in describing the highway itself — narrow roadways, no shoulders or broken ones, too many curves. We may add — few safety railings, few center lines, loose gravel, cramped bridges, unexpected potholes.

By the hazard of things on the road, I do not mean other cars, or trucks and buses. First of all, I mention stones. These may come from landslides, but more commonly they are the result of a custom of the country. Everywhere many of the buses and trucks function on a very narrow margin. The natural place for them to suffer the inevitable breakdown is on a grade. Then, with commendable regard for his own safety, the driver blocks the tires with stones while he is making repairs. Unfortunately, when he drives away, he is likely just to leave the stones there, though they may be within actual sight of one of the innumerable signs against leaving "piedras" on the highway.

Along with "piedras" we must place "ganado," about which many other signs present a warning. *Ganado* must be taken as including all kinds of livestock, from chickens up to horses. (See Picture 26.) These constitute more of a hazard than the stones do. At least you can be sure that a stone is not suddenly going to cross the road ahead of you. From constant practice you become something of an expert in animal-psychology. A burro is more reliable than a horse, and is not likely to come romping onto the pavement at the last moment. A cow is fairly safe, but a calf is not. You learn to keep as far away from the *ganado* as possible, but if they are on both sides of the road, this does not help much. The safe procedure is to keep looking ahead so that you see the animals, and slow down before you get to them. Fortunately more fences are going up all the time, and the trouble with *ganado* is decreasing, except in the more out-of-the-way parts. There the animals still feel that the road is made for their convenience, and I have had a cow lie stolidly in the middle of the pavement in Nicaragua, chewing her cud, and making the car ease its way around her, in spite of all horn-blowing.

To "piedras" and "ganado" we must add "gente." This last — people — is the most dangerous of all. Individuals in the United States are likely to think that highways are made for automobiles; Latin Americans have no such idea. The road is the easiest place to walk, and so they walk there. They may even use the highway for other purposes. (See Picture 29.) Also, when walking, people do not keep to the shoulder. Perhaps there is no shoulder, and in any case the pavement is smoother and easier.

Moreover, unfortunately, man is an uncertain and unpredictable creature. He is much less reliable than the burro, and rates about with the hen, being likely to cross the road suddenly, for no discernible reason. An extra special hazard consists of *el borracho*, the drunk man. "Several for the road" seems to be the rule, and then the road is the highway — often, all of it! But here again, the hazard of Latin America is less than that of the United States. A drunk pedestrian is not nearly as dangerous as a drunk driver, and the small number of cars makes the chances for a drunk driver correspondingly small.

As to driving beyond Mexico City, people ask most of the same questions that they ask about driving to Alaska. First, they inquire, "How about extra gas, spare parts, and more than one extra tire?" All I can say is that I did not carry any, and that I see no great use in doing so. I had to buy an extra tire my last day in Mexico, but I would rather do that than have the nuisance and extra weight of another tire with me all the time.

"Should I be prepared to camp out?" I should definitely say not. There are hotels available, and it is better to stay in one of them. Latin Americans are not used to having tourists camp out, and there might be complications. If I had ever found myself in a fix, I planned to park in some plaza, explain matters to the village police, and spend the night in the car.

There are always those who ask, "Should I carry a revolver?" Many Latin Americans, especially those wealthy enough to own cars, are reputed to carry weapons. For a foreigner to do so only seems to me to be asking for trouble. Also, the question of smuggling a gun — or bribing your way with it — across so many frontiers and then back across all the same frontiers seems to me little short of a nightmare.

This mention of boundary lines brings up the whole matter of customs and immigration inspection. These, at present, constitute as much hindrance to travel as a bad road. (See Pictures 47 and 52.)

First of all, the tourist must spend a lot of time visiting consulates somewhere, waiting in line, filling out forms, and paying fees to get tourist cards or visas so that he can go south, and then from most countries he must do it all over to be allowed to go north.

But all this is just preliminary. At each boundary line you have to stop and pass both customs and immigration, not merely on entering but also on leaving the country. In addition, there are other checking points, and possibly a report to the police or immigration office in the capital city. The number of times we had to pass such inspections, by actual count, was at least sixty-two! I estimate that the total time expended was just about two full eight-hour days. During one day's drive we had to show credentials and fill out forms no less than ten times.

Mexico creates no problem. It is a large country; considering the number of miles the tourist drives through it, he is not stopped an excessive number of times. Like Mexico, Guatemala has a sense of the value of the tourist dollar, and tries to make things easy. The trouble comes in the countries to the south.

The customs inspections are the worst. The inspectors usually insist on your unloading everything, and they paw over your personal belongings. They seldom made any objections to anything. They often seemed to be motivated chiefly by curiosity, being bored, and wanting to see what a tourist was carrying.

The immigration inspections also take a good deal of time, and are the more irritating because they seem more pointless. I got particularly tired of the repeated question "Casado?" I am not ashamed of being married and have no desire to conceal my status, but I simply don't see why it is of such consuming interest to all Central America. The fact of my matrimony must now stand recorded some twenty times in their files.

The officials are friendly and courteous enough, but they are tantalizingly slow, often because they are so nearly illiterate that they read and write with great difficulty. These border stops may even be classed as dangerous, for they involve what may be cruel exposure to the tropical sun, and the environs are often unsanitary.

Something must be done about it if the Central American run is to become popular among American automobilists. I mention the matter, not from a sense of personal irritation, but in the hope that its publication may aid those people in Central America who are working to better the situation. I hope that this section of the book will soon be out-of-date, and of merely historical interest.

This is not a guidebook, and does not give information about hotels. Yet something should be included in a general way on that subject. The situation will have to be improved before tourist travel can increase greatly.

In 1955, accommodations were adequate in Mexico and Guatemala, and since those countries are conscious of the tourist trade, new hotels will probably be built fast enough to keep up with the increased traffic that will come on the completed highway.

South of Guatemala, even with almost no American cars coming through, accommodations were already inadequate. The only good hotels on the line of the highway were in the capitals, and these were so crowded that both in San Salvador and Managua we had to take second-string (though adequate) accommodations. Besides, the run from San Salvador to Managua is too long to be readily made in one day, and that from Managua to San José is also very long. A guidebook lists some hotels in intermediate towns as possible for "emergency accommodations." I took a look at one of these out of curiosity, and found it clean enough and not impossible-looking. As for another of these "emergency accommodations," a local inhabitant remarked, "If you had an open car with the top torn off and it was raining hard, then that would be an emergency in which you might want to use that hotel. Otherwise, better sleep in the car!"

There are, however, excellent locations for intermediate stops. There is lovely highland country near the continental divide in Honduras, and there are locations with views of the sea near Santa Cruz in Costa Rica. One hopes that the tourist bureaus of the various countries will see that good accommodations are available before the tourist rush starts. Otherwise, there will be a great many disgruntled people, and Central America may get a bad reputation.

The comfort and pleasure of driving south vary with the season. From the tourist's point of view we can divide the year into the wet season, the post-wet season, and the dry season.

Books on climatology will inform you that the rains last from May to October, and that the rest of the year is dry. I have added the third season to include the transition time between the conventional wet and dry, and also the first month or so of the dry season.

As with climate in most places, there is variation from year to year. The beginning of the dry season is nothing that you can set your watch by. In addition, there is great local variation with latitude and with altitude and with exposure to winds from the ocean. San Cristóbal, for instance, is much wetter and colder and cloudier than Tuxtla, less than a hundred miles away.

Most people are freer to take their trips in the summer, which is the rainy season along the southern highway. In northern Mexico this means occasional showers, green hills, and — generally speaking — very pleasant weather. You can expect great cumulus clouds piling up on the horizon, and fine opportunities for picture-taking. In central and southern Mexico the rainy season means a violent shower every afternoon, sometimes heavy enough to make driving uncomfortable. In Central America the rainy season means heavy afternoon showers with long drizzles in between, and a great deal of dull sky and low overcast. You can drive for days without ever having any extensive views or seeing the tops of the volcanoes. But the rains keep the weather cooler, lay the dust, and reduce the number of biting insects. Thus, in general, the summer is excellent for Mexico; questionable, though possible, for Central America.

The post-wet season, if you can hit it, is the best of all. In those months, the rains are no longer troublesome, and the country is still fresh and green. In an average year October is excellent for most of Mexico. Farther south the rains continue, and October is counted the worst month of the year in Costa Rica. Still, I was there then, and was able to drive the roads and see the country well enough.

Winter and spring, the full dry season, offer many advantages to the tourist. He is not going to encounter floods and washouts, and the rain will not interfere with his driving or sightseeing. He is able to enjoy extensive views. But he encounters dust, and the blinding sunlight and steady heat become oppressive. Besides, the hills turn brown, and everything dries up into a desert-like aridity. Many of the trees lose their leaves. In the highlands of Chiapas, Guatemala, and Costa Rica, however, the weather remains pleasant, and the country retains some freshness. The dry season is definitely best for those regions.

Residents of most parts of the United States, it may be added, have little to learn and nothing to fear from the weather of Mexico and Central America. A tropical shower furnishes no heavier downpour than that of a Mid-Western thunderstorm. The temperatures, even in the dry season and in the lowlands, are no worse than those of the summer in Chicago or New York. Snow storms and glare-ice are unknown. The worst driving hazard is the fog that may be encountered at high altitudes in the rainy season, and this is not to be feared except at night.

Why drive there? This, at least, is an easy question to answer. In tourist attractions the southern road offers, we may say, just about everything except the Parthenon, Fujiyama, and the Folies Bergères. And it has fairly acceptable substitutes, even for these.

It offers spectacular scenery in amazing variety. I myself had expected a great deal, but found even more than I had expected. Surprising to me, for instance, were the forests with their great individual trees, of many varieties, sometimes scattered across grassy slopes in a park-like beauty which I had always associated with temperate rather than tropical vistas. (See Picture 57.) Wildflowers in profusion, most of them brilliantly colored, also enhance the beauty of such a landscape, at the proper season.

Hunting and fishing offer considerable possibilities, and should become an attraction. There is still game for anyone who wishes to venture a few miles away from the main road. Lake Nicaragua offers the curious possibility of fishing for sharks in fresh water. A hotel-manager in Managua cited these sharks as one of the country's great tourist-attractions. I was not able to follow his reasoning entirely, for they may attract the fishermen, but not the bather. In January, 1956, an American was attacked while swimming in a river near the Costa Rica border, had his leg torn off, and died from loss of blood.

In addition to the doubtful attraction of sharks, however, Mexico and Central America — as already noted — offer almost everything that the tourist can wish. There are the allurements of city-life in the capitals, and the colorful fiestas of the villages. The monuments of the past include every-thing from the ruins of pre-Columbian cities onward. In Mexico one can see sixteenth-century churches constructed in the true Gothic tradition. Some experts believe that the baroque reached its culmination in Mexico and Guatemala rather than in Europe. Mexican architecture still continues to flourish, and as anyone can see by visiting the amazing new university in Mexico City and the residence districts near it. In associations with the historic past, also, the southern road is rich. Some of these are presented in connection with the introductions to the different sectors of the road. A book on the highway, however, must limit itself to that subject and cannot attempt to become a guidebook.

Thus withdrawing to the more restricted subject of the book, this chapter may well end upon the note — and warning — of change. In the next few years anyone attempting to write a guidebook for the highway will find his work becoming obsolete even while he writes. The same is true of parts of this present book. Yet that very fact, in a sense, makes a book more necessary, and a delay would probably not help matters. In the past, the United States has been the great country of the continent for change. Whether the southern republics will alter more rapidly than the United States in the next generation may still be open to question, but in any case they seem likely to become part of that modern world of which change is the most certain quality. Among the factors promoting change, the high-way itself will certainly be one of the most important, and will introduce, for good and for bad, the thronging modern world.

El turismo, as the Latin Americans call it, is a great bringer-in of dollars and a great furnisher of pleasure to millions of people. As such it must be welcomed, and it certainly cannot be denied. Yet *el turismo* is also a great corruptor, and even is likely to kill the thing it loves. Just as the sweeping curves of the highway itself, beautiful in themselves but scarring the hill-sides, impose themselves upon a landscape and make it something different, so also the tourists make something different of the countryside, and of the villages and towns. The cities are less affected; they are large enough to resist the assault, and they are somewhat modernized already.

This change can be rapid. When I drove the as yet unfinished Central Highway of Mexico in 1949, the people were still living in what might be called "pastoral simplicity," much as they had done a hundred years before.

In 1955 the region had become something else, very conscious of tourists. Children had been corrupted into being beggars; boys scrambled about in unseemly competition to wash the car; people and things everywhere had become more modern, which generally means like the United States.

Farther south also, the attitudes of people toward the traveler are determined very much by the length of time tourists have been driving through, and by their numbers. At first, everyone is curious and interested and friendly to see the strangers, but before long this friendliness is likely to be limited to those who are making money from the tourists, and the other inhabitants may develop a kind of resentment.

Only a few years ago, for instance, travelers in Guatemala noted the extreme friendliness of the Indians. The present tourist will more likely feel that they are unfriendly and sullen. This cannot be blamed directly on the highway, which has not yet been finished, but we must remember that Guatemala has been a tourist country for some years. Just what has caused this change is difficult to determine. Certainly the untactful use of the camera has had something to do with it. Some Indians have superstitious objections to having their pictures taken, and in any case it is likely to be taken as an unauthorized invasion of privacy.

South of Guatemala City, where there has been little tourist traffic, the difference is startling. There everyone is smiling and friendly, as they were once reported to have been in the highlands. Inevitably, I am afraid, the change will come.

If there could be some education on both sides, the difficulty might be avoided. Undoubtedly a few of the tourists cause most of the difficulty — by mere untactfulness, and by considering the local inhabitants as exhibits of a zoo. On the other hand, some effort might be made to explain to the local inhabitants that the tourists are only human beings like themselves, mean no harm, and should be accepted in good-humor. Unfortunately, when dealing with large numbers of tourists and inhabitants, education is likely to be a slow process.

But a third stage usually ensues. The inhabitants and the tourists establish a way of getting along together. This has already happened in many of the more tourist-visited countries of Europe, and even, I think, in the vicinity of Mexico City.

By this time, however, the countryside has generally felt the influence of the highway, and the local inhabitant has ceased to be so "picturesque" to the tourist. The old-timer lingers on, and people from the hill-villages continue to come into town, just as nearly naked Indians can still be seen on the thronging streets of modernized Chihuahua. But the highway has brought its inevitable changes. People ride in buses instead of on burros or on trotting little ponies. They start wearing blue jeans instead of white cottons. By then the tourist begins to consider the highway rather old-hat, and to talk of getting "off the beaten track."

Just how soon this will happen along the southern road I cannot say. Even now, it has happened in many places, and change is continuing. But the highway still passes through some "unspoiled country" in Mexico, especially, beyond Oaxaca, and such country still exists everywhere south of Guatemala City. Those who drive the road in the next few years will have to endure some discomforts, but they will also be the more richly rewarded.

THE PAN-AMERICAN HIGHWAY

"As different as north and south" must be written of the roads, not only in a literal sense but in figurative senses as well. Certainly, the two are strikingly different in their histories. The Alaska Highway was a war-baby, pure and simple; the Pan-American, primarily, has been non-military. The former was pushed through in ten months; the latter has been many years a-building. The northern road offers what may well be called an epic of achievement; the southern, a long story of false starts, vacillations, reconsiderations, blunders, and partial failures.

None the less, in one respect at least, the Pan-American Highway — even though not yet completed — represents the more remarkable achievement. Already it stands as a notable example of one of those rarities — an international enterprise, developed chiefly as a peacetime project, by the active cooperation of many sovereign nations. It can thus stand, in most people's minds, as a more admirable monument of human endeavor; in everyone's mind, as a more unusual one.

For, as history goes to show, nations readily unite for common enterprises under the pressure of war, but in time of peace even friendly countries pull apart, because of petty enmities and local jealousies. Therefore, in spite of the blotched record, the people of the United States and of the other nations have a right to be proud of their highway and of their mutual participation in the work of building it. . . .

It is like its northern counterpart, at least, in having many names. It was first called Longitudinal Highway; soon, Pan-American. When the section from the Rio Grande to Panama was conceived as something separate, this was officially designated as the Inter-American Highway. This name, though it came somewhat into ordinary use and is to be found on maps and in some guidebooks, remained essentially a technical term, and did not supplant Pan-American, which was already popularized. As would be expected, wartime rhetoric broke out with such sobriquets as America's Burma Road and Lifeline of the Americas. In Mexico it has been officially designated the Christopher Columbus Highway; in Guatemala, the Franklin D. Roosevelt Highway.

Since most people know it as the Pan-American and since it is by all definitions a part of that highway, the present book uses that term.

Because Mexico has constructed its road-system essentially on a national basis, our account can focus upon Central America. We begin, then, at the opening of that vigorous and imaginative decade of the nineteen-twenties. . . .

At that time the people of the United States were for good roads, about as universally and as normally as preachers were against sin. In the fall of 1920 these good-roads-loving citizens elected as their chief magistrate a man of themselves, to wit, one Warren G. Harding. Since his tenure of office was neither long nor highly glorious, we may at least be happy here to record something to his credit — he may be claimed as the father of the Pan-American Highway.

Whether it was his own idea or came from an adviser, need not be argued. Any chief magistrate picks up ideas where he finds them; the important matter is his advocacy of them. . . . Early in 1921, the President-elect attended a meeting of what was known as the Republican Publicity Association. The matter of rewards and honors being under discussion, one of the loyal party-workers suggested that he himself would like to be minister to Panama. This led to some discussion of Latin America, and to an incidental mention of the possibility of a road to the Canal Zone. Mr. Harding was interested.

This interest endured. Two years later, when the Fifth International Conference of American States was about to be held, the President saw to it that the United States delegation was instructed to look favorably upon suggestions for furthering motor-transportation and highway-building.

Thus the idea was formulated, but throughout the whole decade nothing advanced beyond the idea-stage. Everyone was for good roads, especially if there was no immediate chance of having to pay for them. One gets the idea that nations, in that peaceful decade, had "world enough and time." Attempting to follow developments, one seems to be laboring through a swamp of abstractions, mostly long words embodying *con* and *com*. Congresses and conferences, confederations and conventions, convened; committees consulted and concurred, concluded and recommended, about continental inter-communications and connections in aid of commerce. Lacking from the galaxy, however, were *construction* and even *reconnaissance*.

Gradually the idea, at least, became more precise. The early twenties had thought in vague terms of the general improvement of a system of highways in the Americas. In 1928, however, the Sixth International Conference of American States developed the new plan — at once more practical and more dramatic — of a single north-south road. In a first resolution this project was described by the word Longitudinal, but a second resolution used Pan-American Highway.

At last, on March 28, 1930, the first money was laid on the line, when President Hoover signed a bill appropriating $50,000 for reconnaissance and study.

On June 21, 1930, a party of four men sailed from New York for Panama, to undertake the exploration. Three factors determined the route along which the engineers of the Public Roads Administration must attempt to lay out their line. The highway should serve the more important cities; it should, wherever possible, make use of existing roads; it should adapt itself to the terrain.

Any thought of following the eastern side of the isthmus, along the Caribbean Sea, was quickly eliminated. That coast was not thickly inhabited. Though level, it was crossed by many large rivers, and was swampy and malarial. In addition, a road following this route would by-pass Salvador completely.

The coastal plain on the Pacific side was moderately dry, and not more than moderately unhealthful. A through road, located only with respect to ease of construction and potentialities for handling traffic, should undoubtedly be located on the Pacific plain.

But the locations of the chief cities and the existing roads required that the highway must in some places ascend to the heights and follow along the mountain chain which forms the backbone of the isthmus. This was the general route of the old colonial road or trail known sometimes as El Camino Real. It might be better written *el camino real,* for in no sense was it a unit of the kind that is usually thought worthy of having a proper name. In fact, neither in Central America nor elsewhere should the simple Spanish words be ordinarily given the romantic translation The King's Highway or The Royal Road, even though the words may be literally so interpreted. *El camino real* was "royal" only in the sense that it was conceived as the property of the crown, and so was what we should call a public way, along which any man had a right to pass without restraint of private ownership. At most we can think of it as "the main-traveled road." In ordinary Central American usage, before the automobile era, it seems to have meant the cart road as opposed to the mere pack-trails. Only from the distant past when all the country was under the rule of Spain did some memory descend of a road, or trail, that extended all the way north and south.

Starting with such general data, the reconnaissance parties of the Public Roads Administration entered the field, and during two years were at times as much explorers as surveyors.

In Guatemala, most northerly of the countries to which they were assigned, they found the road-system already somewhat developed. From Guatemala City eastward and northward to Quetzaltenango they could travel by car, and the route which they there determined has since been adjusted only in detail. Beyond Quetzaltenango these first road-locators attempted no final decision, realizing that the point at which the Mexican highway would touch the border was still undetermined. They suggested four possible routes, none of which — incidentally — was destined to be the one finally followed.

East and south of Guatemala City, beyond the famous Esclavos Bridge, two routes were explored. The party first traveled the traditional road, running southwest to Ahuachapán in Salvador. This was passable for cars as far as Jalpatagua, where the party stopped overnight. Beyond that point, they proceeded on muleback. The weather was excessively hot; the dust was deep and powdery; the accommodations at Jalpatagua had been disgusting, nothing other being available than a room in the undertaker's house, from the ceiling of which were suspended ten coffins.

As a result, quite understandably, the road-locators developed an intense dislike for this traverse. Next day, they returned to Guatemala City in a car by way of Santa Ana and Juitapa. They found this route much more to their liking, and selected it for the highway. It was, indeed, longer by twenty miles, and necessitated the crossing of three ranges of hills. On the other hand, it traversed a more populated country. Nevertheless, even the historian of the expedition suggests, with what seems a slight touch of uneasy conscience, that the heat and dust and coffins exercised an influence which "would be hard to estimate."

The exploratory work in Guatemala was accomplished with only one "incident." At San Marcos the party was halted by the police, and found that their hired car was actually a stolen car and that the chauffeur not only lacked a driver's license but also was wanted as a murderer. . . .

In Honduras the location of the road offered few problems, and the highway was routed by the way the *camino real* had always gone, that is, around the heads of the estuaries extending up from the Gulf of Fonseca, through Nacaome and Choluteca, and thence southeast to Nicaragua. Two exciting incidents, however, enlivened the work, and illustrate some of the difficulties of building an international highway.

In Goascorán an inquisitive crowd gathered around the room where the Americans were eating lunch, and peered in at the windows. Suddenly there was commotion. A one-legged old man was struggling through the crowd, frantically waving a large revolver and shouting that it was a shame to sell the country out to foreign interests. He seemed about to take the matter into his own hands. Unfortunately, many members of the crowd apparently thought that he had a very good idea. Eventually he was calmed down, but the surveyors decided to spend the night in Salvador.

A few days later, at San Bernardo, when the party was quietly asleep in the middle of the night, a sudden uproar resounded outside, and the startled Americans, peering out, saw a band of horsemen, armed with what a historian describes as "drawn long-barreled revolvers." Any revolver, one would guess, would have failed to appear "short-barreled" under the circumstances. Soon, however, everything grew quieter. The horsemen turned out to be high-spirited local citizens, who had heard that some foreigners were in San Bernardo, and had thereupon ridden in to discover, in true Wild West fashion, what these strangers were up to. A Honduran representative explained the party's objectives, and all was well. . . .

In Nicaragua, as in Honduras, the party routed the highway to follow the old *camino real*, through Chinandega, León, Managua, Granada, and Nandaime, and thence along the shore of Lake Nicaragua. It traversed easy country, passed through all the larger cities, and was a long-established and (for Central America) a much-traveled road.

Nicaragua, also, supplied its incident. Having set out northward from Chinandega one morning, the party was hastily recalled with the word that sixty Sandinistas (more commonly called "bandits" in local usage) were lying in wait for the Americans. Since these partisans were known to practice decapitation and other plain and fancy methods of disposing of Americans, the party hastily retreated and did not finish its exploration quite to the Honduras line. . . .

The province of Guanacaste, in northern Costa Rica, supplied neither incidents nor difficult problems of location. The party agreed to follow the line of the old trail in general, but considered that some deviation to the east should be made to escape swampy ground close to the Gulf of Nicoya.

But if northern Costa Rica was easy, the southern part of that country was the opposite. In the almost unknown mountains and jungles from Cartago southward the reconnaissance party expended a large proportion of its time and energy in trying to locate a passable route and in mere struggles for existence. On one trip a member overstrained himself, suffered a cerebral hemorrhage, and was with difficulty saved from death. On another occasion the constant irritations of jungle travel so wore upon one man's nerves that he was with difficulty restrained from giving one of his colleagues a thrashing. The surveyors, who at this point really deserve to be called explorers, dared alligators, boa constrictors, and a rare black jaguar. They knew hunger, being forced at times to live off the country as they could, eating wild turkey if they could get it, otherwise making do on monkey meat or on a few fish jerked from a stream. They learned what it was to "sleep with the pigs," and two of them would much have preferred porcine company to that of the two machete-armed dope-smugglers, with whom they were forced to spend one night in a lonely cabin. And remember, if you will, that these men, being permanent government employees, were of the class commonly called "bureaucrats," who are supposed to fatten at public expense in Washington, D.C.

In spite of all their labor the surveyors scarcely succeeded in locating a route in southern Costa Rica. Most of the country was so rough that having got through it at all, the party decided at once that no road could go that way. In the end, however, the highway was actually routed much closer to the old colonial trail than was at first thought could be done. It makes use of the Pass of Death, even though the first surveyors had ruled this out as impossible.

As an example of bureaucracy at work, we can follow in more detail the adventures of the surveyors during a four-day journey which may be considered typical rather than exceptional. At least, on two other occasions they were much closer to extremities than they were on this one.

On April 30, 1931, this group left El Copey, 6250 feet high on the slope of the Talamanca Mountains, about thirty miles by airline south of Cartago, and only three or four miles from the present highway, though on the western instead of the eastern slope. Setting out for San Isidro and points south were five American engineers, mounted on horses, and accompanied by eight *cargadores* each carrying fifty pounds and by four pack-horses with a packer.

They hit the trail at 6.45, and at once faced a steep climb to a cattle-ranch called Las Vueltas at an altitude of over 10,000 feet. The horses were not mountain-bred, and suffered severely. One of them stumbled and fell just at the edge of a 200-foot precipice, and its rider saved himself by slipping off on the inner side. He then quickly sat on the animal's head to prevent it struggling — a ridiculous position for a bureaucrat, who should only sit in a swivel-chair.

From Las Vueltas the trail wound along the crest of the mountains. The end of April should mean the beginning of the dry season, but the high mountains of Costa Rica pay little attention to the calendar. By afternoon, rain was falling in torrents, and the horses were slipping and sliding in the mud. A pack-animal wandered from the trail, stepped into a bog, and went down until little but nostrils and ears were showing. The poor animal was pulled out, but someone's pack was wet.

This incident occurred at a spot almost 11,000 feet high, and the party did not dare risk a night in the open at that altitude. They pushed on, downgrade a thousand feet, to Ojo de Agua, where they had expectations of finding a government rest-house.

They found it, but it was only a small and primitive building, in which six people were already huddling. On a mountain so high that water boiled at too low a temperature to cook beans, everyone went to bed cold and damp and a little hungry.

After a miserable night they were up at dawn. They left Ojo de Aqua by a crazy trail that seemed to go in every direction, including up and down — but mostly up, and very steeply up. It was narrow and dangerous, and ornamented at intervals by crude crosses, each one marking the last breath — or the last step — of some previous traveler. The horses were dispirited and going lame. Occasionally the sun shone, but mostly a thick and cold drizzle seeped down from the sky. At last they left the trees, and came out above timberline, to wind-swept grass-grown summits.

Like most trails along which men have labored with difficulty and danger during many years, this one was marked by many place names, some of them colorful and strange. The Crosses — that was easy enough to understand — and so was the Saints. But the Hill of the Brickmaker's Wife, and the Fandango, and Angel Lake! Soapstone Hill, however, was slippery enough to be descriptive. And then finally El Paso de la Muerte, the Pass of Death, 11,400 feet above the sea!

This was at noon. Beyond the pass the trail went down so steeply that no one dared to ride. It was good judgment, for one horse slipped and fell and rolled, until he lodged between two rocks with his legs waving in the air. This happened quite close to a place where the trail-side was decorated with the skulls and ribs of animals which had died there.

After the horse had been righted and got back to the trail, the mist shifted to rain, again in torrents and even colder than before. It changed to hail, and everyone was close to freezing. The situation was so dangerous that the only remedy was to stop at the next shelter, which bore the understandable but uninspiring name of Casa de la Muerte, "House of Death."

Arrived there, the surveyors were even more surprised than they had been when they found the six men occupying the previous shelter. This one housed a bride and groom! A young couple, newly married near San Isidro, had decided to see the world by taking a wedding trip to San José. To pay for it they were driving a dozen hogs across the mountains to market.

The altitude was 10,650 feet. The hail changed to rain and then back to a mist, drifting in horizontally through the cracks of the poorly built resthouse. Two of the Americans put up a tent, but everybody else crowded into the little house along with the bride — which reminds us of the radio-announcer's blooper about a rendition of "*My Lady Sleeps* — with a male chorus."

Came the dawn, and a breakfast of coffee and oatmeal, only half-cooked, because of the altitude. At six the party said good-bye to the bride and groom and the pigs, and went off in "very cold" weather, on a trail that went up and down the crest along the ridge — but, this day, mostly down. The descent grew steeper until the horses were no longer sure of their footing, and the men had to dismount. Animals and men alike were getting to the end of their strength. One of the engineers tried to mount again at a level spot, but was unable to do so, and had to rest half an hour before going on. They were coming down through trees again now.

At last they arrived at a little hillside plantation, and managed to get eggs and coffee, the best meal they had had in more than three days. In heavy rain, they continued to descend during the afternoon. They spent the night at a place which we may translate as Lower Fairview, in the one-room house of one of their own carriers, along with the man, his wife, a large family of children, and an uncounted number of dogs, cats, pigs, chickens, and ducks. The place had an earthen floor, which became a mingling of mud and filth because of the goings and comings of the pigs and ducks, which showed no objection to sallying out for a stroll in the rain. The altitude, however, was low enough so that the night was not too cold, and the exhausted Americans had a good sleep, in spite of the livestock.

Next day, the sky was clear and the air cool and brisk. The trail wound easily down the valley and across the rolling hills. By 10 A.M. the party made San Isidro. Both horses and men were so exhausted that a rest of two days had to be ordered before the expedition continued to the south.

Until June, 1933, the work of reconnaissance was vigorously pursued. Aerial photography was used to supplement the information so laboriously gained on the ground. The result was the location of a practicable line for a highway in all the Central American countries except Salvador, which was already developing the road on its own initiative.

With preliminary reconnaissance thus expeditiously completed, one would like to record that further work proceeded at once. Actually, it did not. By 1933 the United States was economically groggy, and expensive undertakings in foreign countries could no longer be considered. Moreover, the diplomats had to clear the way before the engineers could really begin. The Latin American has often harbored a fear of the Colossus of the

North bearing gifts. Costa Rica, in particular, had reason to be suspicious of an American-dominated road. Could she not see, to the south, Panama with American troops in the Canal Zone; to the north, American marines in Nicaragua?

At this point, then, while the history of the highway itself pauses, we may take the time to consider the numerous "stunt" journeys, most of them inspired by the publicity accorded the highway.

Who first had the specific idea of traveling overland between the two Americas, or even from the United States to Panama? In colonial days, indeed, after Gonzago Vásquez had opened his trail from Cartago to Chiriquí in 1601, anyone sufficiently energetic could certainly have traveled all the way from New Mexico to Panama, largely by ox-cart and elsewhere by mule-back. With economic and political disintegration, with revolutionary wars, banditry, and renewed Indian truculence, what was possible in the early seventeenth century had become — practically speaking — impossible in the nineteenth century.

The beginning of the twentieth century offered quieter times, and from the year 1902 dates the first such attempt that I have found. In that year Hans Gadow, journeying between Tehuantepec and Oaxaca, met two Catalan Spaniards who were walking from Mexico City to Buenos Aires. I know of no other record of these two.

In the second decade of the century the Mexican Revolution and the World War discouraged such attempts. By 1925, however, everything was quieter, and the agitation for a highway had started people thinking about an overland journey. A great many were attempted, with more or less success. We can at least list them briefly, and thus demonstrate their variety.

In 1927 A. F. Tschiffely, who had come north from Buenos Aires, traveled with two Argentine ponies from Panama through the difficult jungle country of southern Costa Rica to Puntarenas. Having traversed the most difficult section, he lost his chance to make a complete overland journey to the United States when revolutionary conditions in Nicaragua forced him to take ship to La Unión in El Salvador. Thence he continued by horseback to Washington.

In 1927 a certain Augusto Flores, nationality unknown, was in Panama. He said that he was walking through on a wager. He was later reported in

Nicaragua, and finally in New York, but there is no proof that he went overland all the way.

José Mario Barone, an Italian, made the first attempt to drive a car from South America to the United States. Early in 1927 he left Rio, and he arrived in New York after a trip which consumed more than two years and cost the lives of two men. Even from Panama he was not able to make a continuous journey, but shipped his car at least twice by boat.

In 1930 Joseph and Arthur Lyons, of Nevada, left New York in a Ford car equipped to run on railroad tracks. They reached Managua, thus establishing a record for continuous automobile travel toward the south. One may question, however, whether a car able to run on rails still retains its amateur standing.

An expedition of three Brazilians had left Rio in 1928, under the leadership of Leonidas Borges de Oliveira, traveling in two Model-T's. They experienced many adventures, suffered accidents, and were sometimes in financial difficulties. They arrived at Panama City in June, 1932. From northern Panama rumors came back that they had taken their cars apart, to transport them across country on mule-back. They got to Washington in 1937, after nine years! They had made an astounding journey, and received much acclaim in the United States. Nevertheless, they were unable to satisfy a critical investigator that they had not resorted to shipping their cars in places, and according to the best authorities the section between Panama and Costa Rica, at least, was impassable.

Though they had started at a comparatively early date, the Brazilians spent so much time on the road that even before they reached Panama much exploration had already been accomplished to the northward. In 1931, for instance, the expedition sponsored by the Automobile Club of Southern California had driven from the United States into Central America. These well-equipped and tough professionals could certainly have gone farther south, but they had expended so much time in southern Mexico that they did not go on beyond San Salvador. (See pp. 97 and 123.)

In 1935 G. P. Peck and E. W. James drove the first car from Panama City to the frontier of Costa Rica, with the aid of block-and-tackle and improvised ferries. They then flew to San José, and thence traveled by road as much as possible, but resorted to airplane or steamer three times.

In 1936 two Argentines, Vicente Escasa and Victor Saraffia, arrived in

Washington, having ridden most of the way from Buenos Aires on a tandem bicycle.

In May, 1936, two young Venezuelans, Rafael Petit and Juan Carmona, passed through Panama on foot. Thirteen months later they arrived at the usual goal of Washington, telling a circumstantial story which inspired confidence that they had walked the whole way.

In *The Pan American Highway,* published in 1940 and illustrated with many photographs, Harry A. Franck and Herbert C. Lanks recorded their recent journey to the south, along the line of the highway, in so far as was then possible. These veteran travelers in Latin America used public transportation.

Another interesting trip — and about the last to be considered in the pioneering class — was that of Sullivan C. Richardson and two companions in 1940-41, described in his *Adventure South.* This expedition managed to make a dry-season drive clear to San José in Costa Rica.

These journeys demand one general comment. Although the people of the United States consider themselves highly energetic and adventurous, most of these explorers — and all the more daring ones — came from the south! Are we actually less in the tradition of Boone and Crockett than we like to think?

In addition to the more-or-less authenticated journeys, many others were planned, and some of these were partially accomplished. As might be expected, moreover, the whole subject breaks down eventually into hearsay, rumor, and folktale. E. W. James, who has assiduously collected and sifted the stories, admits that at least two of these people were real, even if their journeys cannot be authenticated.

One of them was the Swedish (or Danish) woman, said to have walked from the United States to Panama, chaperoned by a German police dog. She actually addressed a woman's meeting in the Canal Zone. Indians south of the Canal later reported having been visited by a white woman with a dog.

James himself saw the man with the four-horned sheep. Both man and sheep were real, but the man seemed as mad as Hieronimo, and James could not trust his story of an overland march. In any case, he claimed to have come from the south, and is not known to have gone farther north than Panama.

Let us merely list the other interesting overlanders — real or fabulous —

of whom James heard tales. Most of these specialized in the transit from South America to Panama, but just where any of them actually went is doubtful enough.

(1) A Catholic priest who walked from Buenos Aires to New York, doing a little missionary work among the Indians on the side,

(2) A German taxidermist and his Negro assistant,

(3) A young man from Hagerstown, Maryland,

(4) A Czechoslovak who afterward went native and lived in the jungle, so wild that he could not even be coaxed into camp to tell his story,

(5) A Chinese smuggler,

(6) An itinerant Syrian,

(7) A whole motley company of mining prospectors, timber cruisers, and what you will.

To sum up, down to 1940, no overland trip between Panama and the United States can be fully authenticated, although it is very likely that the two Venezuelans actually got through on foot.

Returning from this fearsome assemblage of women with police dogs, mad Czechoslovaks, and young men from Hagerstown, Maryland — we again take up the mundane story of construction.

In 1934 the United States appropriated a million dollars. These were the days of the New Deal, and this is to be conceived as a pump-priming project. By arrangement with the Central American countries, the money was to be expended for supplies in the United States, and the countries through which the highway passed were to supply labor. The Public Roads Administration set up an office in Central America, and prepared to supervise the work. Not a great deal could be done with the money available, and it was decided to concentrate on bridges. The first three to be undertaken were those over the Chiriquí in Panama, the Choluteca in Honduras, and the Tamazulapa in Guatemala.

Work on the greatest of these, the Choluteca Bridge, began on April 15, 1936. Good local masons were available, and much stone was used. With the usual Latin-American love of finish and elaboration, the Honduran government insisted that some of this stone work should be artistically carved. The project was a fine example of international cooperation. The United States furnished technical assistance, cement, steel, and machinery for work. Honduras furnished sand and stone, lumber, gasoline, and labor. Common laborers received fifty cents a day; carpenters, $1.00; masons, $1.12½. Delivery of supplies proved one of the most difficult parts of the job. These had to be handled, with many transhipments, by lighter and truck, and even by ox-carts and the large dugout canoes called *bongos.*

Slowly the superstructure arose — two suspended spans of 330 feet each, plus back stays of 110 feet — a total length of 1088 feet, comparable to the Lower Liard bridge on the Alaska Highway or the suspension bridge across the St. Lawrence at Montreal. The whole was completed on November 11, 1937.

In the meantime, Costa Rica and Nicaragua, though at first they had held back, had come in on the arrangement. By June 30, 1938 — remarkable how far a million went in those days! — fifteen bridges had been built, many of them over considerable rivers, and others had been surveyed and designed. Unfortunately, no comparable advance was made in road construction, so that these magnificent structures stood up like monuments in the wilderness with very inferior roads leading off from either end.

By this time a good many changes had been made in the original location of the road, as it had been worked out in the early thirties. At the north, the entrance from Mexico was to be made via Tapachula, though from the frontier the road had to climb up from nearly sea-level to an 8000-foot pass, steeply and around countless bad curves.

The most important change of location was in Nicaragua, where the route had indeed been wholly shifted from the traditional one, except for the fifty miles at the southern end. As a result of the insistence of the Nicaraguan government, the projected line of the highway had left the direct and almost water-level line, to climb circuitously over mountains. Not only did this shift make the road longer and much more difficult for through traffic, but also it was unfortunate from the tourist's point of view. He was thus forced to pass through many miles of undistinguished hill-country and to miss seeing the most highly cultivated and historically interesting part of Nicaragua. This region around the ancient city of León, because of its "fruits and fertility," had been described by Thomas Gage as "the Paradise of America."

The change was to some extent based upon a reasoning which was logical, at least from the Nicaraguan point of view. If constructed along the traditional route, the new road would parallel an already constructed railroad, thus giving double facilities to that region while other parts of the republic were left wholly without communication.

This objection to having railways and highways run parallel has appeared also in other countries. Superficially it may seem to rest upon sound logic, but its reasonableness may be doubted. Because of ease with which supplies can be hauled, a highway can often be built more cheaply when close to a railroad. Thus built, moreover, the two lend each other mutual support — a matter of real moment in countries where both floods and earthquakes are common and often block communications.

At this time an even more extreme minor contortion was also forced upon the road in Nicaragua. This took it from Sébaco to Matagalpa and then through Jinotega to Estelí, instead of directly to Estelí. This quirk, through forty additional miles of mountainous country, was necessitated by the desire of the then president of the republic to have the road pass by some land that he owned.

These shifts in Nicaragua also necessitated a relocation through mountainous country in Honduras, from the border to Choluteca.

In 1941, just before the United States entered the war, the Public Roads Administration was able to announce that of the estimated 3252 miles of highway from the Rio Grande to Panama City 2004 miles was "all-weather." This sounded better than it actually was, for in this year one could not drive even as far as Oaxaca on a decent road. Beyond the impassable regions of southern Mexico, the 300-mile stretch across Guatemala was rated as all-weather, but it was actually a mountainous and second-rate affair, even dangerous. Salvador had its section in good shape. Farther south, however, there was little possibility of continuous travel. In fact, the PRA also announced, "highway travel is largely a short-distance movement." An explanation was added that the Central American countries were naturally more interested in building roads to serve their own local needs than in a single through highway.

In spite of such plain warnings the idea was already wide-spread that the road to Panama and even South America was, so to speak, just around the corner. Optimistic magazine articles fostered this belief. Kipling was put under heavy requisition and within a single year the popular magazines offered not only "Rolling down to Rio," but also "Rolling down to Panama," and "Roll on to Buenos Aires."

The approach of war brought renewed interest in the highway, and just after Pearl Harbor the President signed a bill appropriating $20,000,000 to be expended in cooperation with the Central American countries.

Just as the military need of a road to Alaska came to be recognized in the early months of 1942, so it was to the south. In strategic importance Panama at least equaled Alaska. Early in 1942, the Japanese were in a position to threaten communications between the Canal Zone and the United States on the Pacific side. At the same time, the German submarine campaign was almost severing the Atlantic communications.

The two operations of road-building, north and south, might well have been conceived as a single operation; actually, the southern road took second place. The decision to build the Alaska Highway may even have worked against the road to Panama. Statesmen and generals might well ask, "If we are going to put our energy into building roads, as purely defensive operations, how are we going to be able to mount an offensive?"

Nevertheless, the Services of Supply, most immediately concerned with the momentous and difficult task of munitioning the Canal Zone, insisted that the road should be built. Other military authority was in opposition — in particular, interestingly enough, the man who more than a decade later was to support the highway and sign the bill making its completion possible. This was the Assistant Chief of Staff, a comparatively unknown major-general named Eisenhower.

With the Army thus divided, the bulldozers were already tearing at the northern muskeg before any decision was reached about the southern road, and directives for its building were not issued until June, 1942, after the battle of Midway had removed all threat to the Pacific communications. In fact, one may say that the Army never really did make up its mind, and as a result, figuratively speaking, resorted to tactics which have been disastrous on many a battlefield — sending a battalion to do a brigade's work.

The decision was made to build the highway, but the operation was not granted a high priority. No engineering regiments were assigned to the task. The construction was to be done by contractors under the direction of the Engineers and the Public Roads Administration, depending chiefly upon local labor. Nevertheless, the original directives called for the closing of all gaps by the construction of a pioneer road to be completed in *one* year!

Even under the best circumstances the schedule would have been difficult to keep, and with low priorities it was impossible.

The work began bravely enough. In September a dispatch from San José stated: "Hundreds of engineers and thousands of laborers have begun work on various sections of the Pioneer Road." Drawn to the inevitable cliché the dispatch called it "the Burma road of Central America." This dispatch with its easy mention of hundreds and thousands was optimistic, but at least the greatest activity and the most successful construction was in Costa Rica. Under the supervision of the Public Roads Administration, the very difficult Talamanca Mountains were conquered. By the old route over the Pass of Death, where the first reconnaissance party had found the bridal couple and the pigs, the new road was blasted and bulldozed clear to San Isidro. Even this stretch, however, was not completed until 1945.

Elsewhere the work proceeded under direct Army supervision, and it is not too much to say that in this engagement, the army — at least its Corps of Engineers — suffered one of its worst defeats of history. With low priorities, many contractors would not submit bids at all, and those who did regretted it. Almost immediately everyone realized that even a scratched-out pioneer road could not be finished in a year, and the proposed date of completion was postponed until June, 1944.

Long before this second date was reached the Army had washed its hands of the whole project. Late in 1943 the work was abandoned, and the great amounts of expensive machinery which had been transported from the United States were left to rust.

The conclusions of a post-war Senatorial investigating committee were scathing. As a war-effort the project was viewed as having accomplished considerably less than nothing, that is, millions of dollars had been spent and much time and material consumed "without contributing to the defense of the United States."

After the Army withdrawal, work continued on the San Isidro road and did not altogether lapse elsewhere. The PRA, which had been concerned with the road long before the Army's sudden flurry, continued its interest. Its report for 1945 noted that work continued, "but only at a moderate pace." In 1946 also "moderate progress" was noted, but by 1947 the comment was: "seriously hampered by lack of funds." The 1949 report stated that the work was practically at a standstill. This period of complete slump continued for several years.

In the meantime, optimistic writers for magazines and newspapers completed the road yearly and almost monthly. All during the war people had heard vaguely about the road being built to Panama, and they knew that a road had been completed to Alaska. Being citizens of the United States, they supposed that any project undertaken would be completed before very long. Apparently the editors thought the same, or else decided that people should hear what they wanted to hear. In any case, "road to be completed *next year*" was repeated every year. As in 1941, the titles of many articles suggested that you could already make the drive. A 1949 contribution was "Shall we motor to Alaska or to the Argentine?" A study of the indexes reveals some interesting sequences. *Time* published "Panama by '49," and then "Panama by '50." Eventually, however, that magazine became cynical, and a third title was "Panama by '59?"

In these same years automobile clubs, travel bureaus, and even the PRA were deluged with inquiries about driving through Central America. Many set out to do so. There was a revival of stunts. People tried it by all sorts of methods. As before the war, there was a rash of those who claimed to have driven all the way through, but became vague when asked how they got across the gaps — the one at the Mexico-Guatemala border, and the two in Costa Rica. Occasional cars even overcame the first two of these. One jeep managed to make it across from Comitán to Huehuetenango, following the trails. Some cars got through from Arriaga to Tapachula, in the dry season, as the Automobile Club of Southern California expedition had done in 1931. Three young men from California, in an amphibious jeep, traveled along the sand spits of the barrier islands in that area, boldly taking to the water to pass the gaps between islands. As a few other cars also managed, they went through Guanacaste, though at one point they broke down and had to be hauled by ox-team.

As far as I have ascertained the record, however, only one man actually journeyed overland, keeping fairly close to the line of the highway, all the way to Panama, and he was often forced to employ — in his own phrase — "Shank's mare."

This was Roger Stephens — fifty-seven years old when he made the most difficult part of the journey, a retired advertising man, on a tight budget, poorly equipped, in no better physical condition than would be expected for one of his age and profession. His success is an indication of how much can be accomplished by a determined man who merely keeps going ahead.

Yet there was certainly an element of luck too. At several points Stephens was close not only to failure, but also to disaster and death. He was a man of innumerable whims and fancies, some helping and some hindering his journey. Many of the Central Americans he encountered must have considered him mad, and probably this encouraged them to take better care of him than they would have done otherwise. He would eat no meat, and would apparently drink nothing alcoholic. He would kill nothing, not even a poisonous snake. He was so pitiful of animals that he generally led his horse over all the hard places, and mounted only to ford streams and when the going was easy.

Physically, he strained himself to the breaking point. On one of the mountain trails when he was crossing between Mexico and Guatemala he suffered sunstroke, but he continued after a brief rest. In the Costa Rica jungle he almost regularly collapsed at the end of the day, dropping by the trail when the village marking the end of the march finally came into sight, and lying there half an hour or so until he felt able to continue.

He had, moreover, no sense of equipment. As his sole water-supply he toted an awkward and heavy vacuum bottle, holding only a quart.

He did not ease his hardships by spending money, for he nursed an obsession to make the trip as cheaply as possible, and he recorded every penny expended. When he occasionally had to hire a taxi, his journal seems to scream with anguish.

He had a good-enough knowledge of Spanish, and greatly enjoyed his contacts with the people. Otherwise, he was by no means an exuberant or joyous traveler, and was ridden by myriad fears. He could not take a step on the trail without fearing to tread on a snake, or let anything pass his lips without worry about amoebas.

As for his means of travel, anything went — so long as it was by land, and followed the line of the highway, and was cheap. He preferred second-class buses, or getting a free ride with somebody who happened to be going his way. Renting a private car was too expensive, and riding a horse was too cruel. So, in the hard places, he generally noted, "Shank's mare."

But he got through.

During this period a change of administrations in Nicaragua permitted the elimination of the scandalous Matagalpa loop. Even more important was a change of location farther north.

The Mexico-Guatemala connection had always caused trouble, and the

Army had added a disturbing factor by rejecting the difficult climb up to San Marcos, and adopting a route from Tapachula along the coastal plain of Guatemala. By 1946, however, Mexico had pushed its road as far as Comitán, and anyone looking at a map could see that the direct road from that town to Guatemala City would be a great deal shorter if it proceeded directly through the highlands.

As a result, the route through the gorge of the Selegua River was adopted. This affected a saving, overall, of 93 miles, and eliminated much of the descent from the highlands and the climb back. Unfortunately, this saving in distance was entirely in favor of Mexico, which had an active highway program. The length of highway in Guatemala was actually increased a little, and that republic, which had been a leader in the early thirties, had by the late forties become a laggard. Moreover, road-construction through the Selegua Gorge offered great difficulties, and was of no local importance. Besides, the Guatemalans had already opened a road to the Mexican border at one point, and had a feeling that they had done their share. Finally, the whole situation in that country was becoming less favorable, because of the assumption of power by a government unfriendly to the United States.

Mexico completed its road to the border in 1950, and there the pavement dead-ended against a brush-choked ravine. Then things rested in one of the most exasperating situations ever to be experienced in the history of highways. There was a road through Mexico to the border, and there was a road through Guatemala to the border, but they reached the border at points separated by about a hundred miles.

At that time the United States was engaged in the Korean war, and had many commitments in Asia and Europe. There was little interest in spending money to complete a road in Central America. Nevertheless Congress appropriated $4,000,000 in 1951, and Costa Rica continued to work steadily at closing the Guanacaste gap. In 1952 $12,000,000 was appropriated for the next biennium, but in this same year conditions in Guatemala became so bad that the PRA abandoned its office there. The best that the PRA report for 1953 could announce was that thirty miles had been completed in Guanacaste. A little work had been done on the highway in Salvador and Nicaragua; none at all in Guatemala and Honduras.

Even in this year a considerable number of American cars were still trying to get through Central America. This was, however, about the end of such attempts. In 1955, I saw very few American license plates, and these were generally on cars which had been brought home by returning Central Americans, or else had been brought there for business purposes. I actually talked to not a single tourist who was in his own car, and in San Isidro my license plates were the subject of much curiosity.

After a change of regime in Guatemala, the agreement between that country and the United States was renewed, on September 2, 1954. With a slightly increased appropriation, activity was resumed in that country. Costa Rica was steadily working ahead in Guanacaste. In Salvador the road was now nearly all paved. In Nicaragua about half of the road was "black-top," and the rest was "all-weather," much of it graded up to Pan-American standards. In Honduras the road was mostly good gravel, but there were a few uncertain miles near the Nicaragua frontier, including one ford where a car might be stalled in wet weather.

In February, 1955, Vice-President Nixon visited Central America on a good-will tour. To anyone traveling in those countries, the need of the highway becomes obvious, and the anomaly of its near-completion could not help but make an impression. The highway represented for the United States an investment into which a good many million dollars had poured, and yet this investment could not really pay dividends until a little more money had been expended. Mr. Nixon was quick to see the possibilities, and his chief agreed. In April, President Eisenhower asked Congress for an appropriation, arguing in its support the economic development of Central America, trade and political relations, tourist travel, and security.

On May 7, while the bill was under consideration, the Guanacaste Gap was finally closed and that highway was officially opened, without much fanfare in the United States, but in the presence of one of our senators and five congressmen.

On July 1, 1955, President Eisenhower signed a bill appropriating $75,000,000, to complete the highway to Panama in three years. The general understanding with the Central American countries — except Salvador, which was not involved — was that each was to contribute about half as much again as the United States expended within their borders. Naturally, the Selegua Gap, "El Tapón," was to have high priority. By October, contracts had been let to different American companies to open the road through to the Mexican border, and work had already been begun.

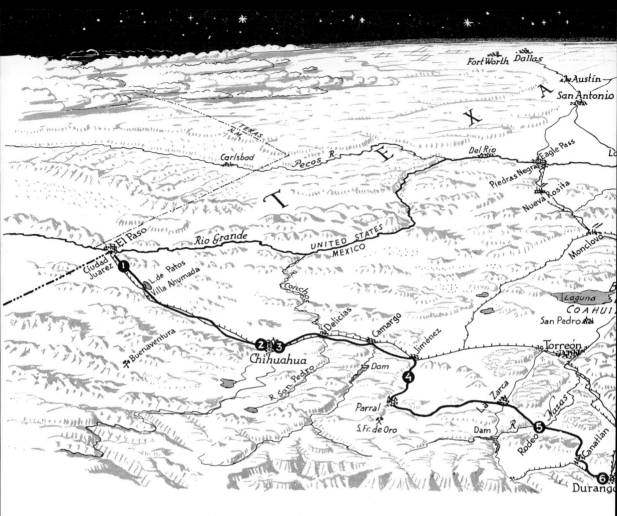

KING'S ROAD OF THE INTERIOR
Ciudad Juárez to Mexico City

From border to capital the ribbon of pavement leads on for 1325 miles. The route includes the whole of Mexico 45, and then for the last hundred miles follows Mexico 85, the original Pan-American Highway extending south from Laredo. This section has a unity of its own, both geographically and historically. It has not even lacked a name, having been known in colonial times as El Camino Real de la Tierra Adentro, the King's Road of the

Interior. It is now generally distinguished as the Central Highway, although official Mexican usage allows the name Pan-American to be applied to all of the chief roads extending south from the border.

In spite of its length this whole section is so much of a unit that it is better described as a whole than broken into parts.

All the way the road follows the north-south trend of the Mexican plateau, and keeps high. Even the lowest point, at Ciudad Juárez on the Rio Grande, is 3700 feet above sea-level. Farther south, the road maintains a general level more than a mile high, passing a summit of over 8000 feet near

Zacatecas. Yet, on the whole, there is little impression of altitude. Since the level of the plateau itself is so high, its bordering mountains fail to dominate it, though some of them rise to 10,000 feet.

The land, as far as the automobilist is concerned, is one of broad-stretching valleys separated by rolling hills or low mountains. In the valleys the road reaches far ahead, straight and inviting. "The tangent," on both sides of La Zarca, is a 35-mile straightaway, without curve or important hill. Passing from valley to valley, the road winds through broken country, and in a few places climbs sufficiently to give some impression of mountain-driving. But the ordinary car will seldom be out of high gear. These hilly sections, in fact, serve chiefly to lend variety to the driving.

The alternation of valley and hills also expresses itself in the shifts back and forth between dry sterility and rich cultivation. After leaving the irrigated districts near Ciudad Juárez, the tourist passes across two-hundred miles of country which closely approaches the sandy waste of Arabia and the Sahara. Only when he has driven close to three hundred miles and enters the Conchas Valley, near Ciudad Delicias, does he see a second richly cultivated area, again as the result of irrigation. Farther south, however, the summer rainfall increases, and corn (as almost everywhere in Mexico) is the prevailing crop. El Bajío, the broad valley stretching around Celaya, is one of the richest in all Mexico. Even the hill country, toward the south, is not wholly unproductive, but produces a little corn and maguey, and everywhere offers pasturage for cattle.

The contrast between upland and valley is reflected in human habitation. The hill country is empty. One may drive for miles without seeing a person, and gasoline stations are many miles apart. At best, the road encounters some poor village of adobe huts. But each valley has its city or large town and its broad expanse of cultivated fields.

Partly because of agriculture in the valleys, partly as the result of old-time mining ventures, the highway passes through a well-spaced succession of cities. Most of these date back several centuries, and still maintain a "colonial" character, side by side with bustling modern developments. Zacatecas is one of the most picturesque cities of the continent. Such another is Guanajuato, which lies a few miles off the highway but within easy reach. Chihuahua, Durango, Aguascalientes, León, Celaya, Querétaro — all are typical and notable Mexican cities. In fact, this succession of cities serves to provide a distinctive interest to the route.

By and large, indeed, even though scenically somewhat monotonous, it is a delightful road for the sheer joy of driving. Traffic is not heavy, and the adaptation of the highway to the land is always a source of pleasure. There are no billboards. Lacking though it may be in major scenic attractions the Central Highway serves as a proper introduction to Mexico.

Historically, this road is by far the most interesting of the three which now lead southward from the United States. The road from Laredo, though it was the original Pan-American, is chiefly a modern creation dating from the 1930's. The West Coast Highway, also, may be called a historical side-road. But the King's Road of the Interior follows the main-line route by which the Spaniards worked northward in search of silver to mine and of souls to save, and much Mexican history is involved with it.

The first rush of Cortez and his *conquistadores* reached north as far as Querétaro. Their halt in that region, which they occupied in 1531, was not the result of any opposition of the natives. It was simply that beyond Querétaro there was nothing worth conquering. Northward no rich and civilized Indian cities lured the Spaniards on, and the arid uplands were occupied by only a few naked and dirty savages, who did not even depend upon cultivating corn, but wandered about, eating snakes and rats and anything else they happened to catch. Even the rich valley to the west of Querétaro — that one later to be called the Bajío — was held by these miserable ones.

Without regard to niceties of ethnology, the Spaniards called all these tribes Chichimecas. This was an Aztec term, a derogatory one, meaning "dirty dogs" or something of that sort. But primitive though they were and few in numbers, the Chichimecas were vicious, cruel, aggressive, and thoroughly tough fighters. They used powerful bows, and were disconcertingly skillful at shooting their obsidian-tipped arrows. Armed with clubs and stone-hatchets, they did not flinch from hand-to-hand combat.

So the Spaniards occupied Querétaro to the north, and went out west from Mexico City to veer northwestward and seize the region around Guadalajara, but the Chichimecas held the Bajío and also extended off to the north, no one knew how far. So things remained throughout all the later part of the 1530's and on to the next decade. During these years Coronado and other Spaniards explored by circuitous routes to very distant regions, but no one entered the Chichimeca country. So it happens, curiously, that the Spaniards knew about the region that was to be the far-off state of Kansas before they knew about the region that was to be the close-by state of Guanajuato.

During these years there existed only what may be called the first section of the Central Highway, from Mexico City north to Querétaro. It came up through Jilótepec to San Juan del Río, and for part of the way there was an alternate route through the ancient city of Tula. No important modern road passes from Mexico City to San Juan by that route, but from San Juan to Querétaro, about thirty miles, Mexico 45 follows the ancient route very closely, and in this region you still see many evidences of old roads, though the actual remains cannot go back to Aztec times, or even to the very first years of Spanish occupation.

Before long, however, some Spaniards were certainly going to set about penetrating what might well have been called the Wild North. Two great attractions — irresistible attractions, one might say — were pulling them on. One of these, a desire to discover mines of gold and silver, is easy enough for the modern mind to appreciate. The other, a desire to convert souls to True Church, is harder for most of us to appreciate, but it was passionately strong in the Spanish missionaries. Characteristically, the first important expedition northwards included both prospectors and friars.

This party, commanded by Captain Juan de Tolosa, set out from Guadalajara. Tolosa had with him a few Spanish horsemen, four friars, and some Indians from a local tribe that the Spaniards had already conquered. The year was 1546, and they started in the late summer, which would be a good time for exploring in that region, what with the rain easing off but the grass being high enough to afford good grazing for the horses. The real jumping-off place was Juchipila, forty miles north of Guadalajara, where they probably recruited, or conscripted, most of their Indians. From there they quite possibly followed the line of an easy opening in the hills, northeastward, and came out into a broad valley with some hot springs in it. They would have called the springs *aguas calientes,* and from that simple description we have later the name of the city and the state. From the hot springs, if Tolosa really went that way, he and his men would have gone north, following along the present line of Mexico 45.

Whatever way they went, they must have moved slowly. All but a few of them were on foot, and many of the Indians were plodding along under heavy packs. Doubtless the party was under way at daybreak, ready to halt before the afternoon shower sent the water rushing down the gullies, and also ready to halt early so that they could be sure of getting a defensible camp-site. During the march the horsemen presumably scouted around, learning the lay of the land, looking for outcroppings that might indicate silver ore, and even examining the streambeds for colors of gold.

After some days of traveling toward the north, they must have begun to notice a striking landmark far ahead. It was a mountain, showing at its very top a high and long outcropping of greenish-gray rock, looking a little like a flattish cockscomb or the cropped mane of a horse. (Driving northward from Aguascalientes, the tourist can still see this landmark, even when it is miles away.)

Tolosa may well have directed his march toward it consciously, realizing that in its vicinity there would be a good chance for prospecting. Also, his Indians may have told him that he would find there an encampment of Chichimecas who would be able to give him information.

Certainly, he marched there, and at his arrival, the Chichimecas rushed from their encampment, and fled to their stronghold on the mountain, clear at the top of the great greenish-gray outcropping.

Tolosa was not looking for trouble. He had with him some Indians who spoke the local language, and he sent them to parley. He made use of the usual, but generally hypocritical, approach of Europeans to natives in such a situation, declaring that he was peacefully inclined, and offering presents. After a while the fugitives were convinced, and doubtless being very curious about the Spaniards and their horses, and wanting presents, they came down from their rock. Being given the usual trinkets, they were delighted, and gladly rushed about bringing specimens of rock. There is a possibility that some of these Indians had been captives and slaves of the Spaniards at one time, and knew what silver ore was.

Before long the Spaniards' eyes lighted up with the glow of cupidity. On September 8, 1546, Tolosa located his claim for a silver mine, not far from the foot of the landmark mountain.

By their actions the Chichimecas, in the usual foolish fashion of savages, had contrived their own destruction, for once a Spanish mining settlement had been established in their country, they were in for trouble, no matter what promises had been made to them.

In the next few years the mines were opened, and proved to be fabulously rich. Curiously, the great rush came in 1549, so that there were Forty-niners in Mexico just three hundred years before the Forty-niners of California.

Since the Chichimecas of that region were of a tribe calling themselves Zacatecos, the town that grew up there was called Zacatecas, and it bore on its coat of arms a figure of the Virgin, whose birthday is celebrated on September 8. In some way the greenish-gray outcropping came to be called La Bufa, a word meaning "pig's bladder" in Basque, though it looks nothing like a bladder. The name may actually be derived from some Indian word.

When there was a rich mining-strike, well-established trails to it seemed to spring up overnight. The original approach had been from Guadalajara, and soon two trails led from that city to Zacatecas. One of these, from Aguascalientes north, followed the general line of the present highway. From the settlements of Michoacan another trail led to the mines, and this one came up across the Bajío, thus establishing the route of the present highway from Silao on. Naturally, however, the most important road was that which led from Mexico City. It made use of the already established trail as far as Querétero, and then led on northwestwards across high barren country, not approaching the present line of the highway except for the few miles just south of Zacatecas.

The sudden development of so many routes may seem surprising, but it is not really to be wondered at, and it is in fact very illustrative of the nature of the country, which is one of the easiest possible for communications. There are no thick forests or barrier mountains, and the rivers can be forded, except after flash floods in the rainy season. A horseman or even a packtrain can go anywhere, and a skillful teamster should be able to drive an ox-cart between any two points with only a little exercise of ingenuity at finding a route. One remembers that the American pioneers took their covered wagons all the way to Oregon and California. A Mexican ox-cart is a good deal more maneuverable than a covered wagon, and the Mexican plateau offers fewer difficulties than the Rocky Mountains. Besides, the continuing richness of the Zacatecas mines was so astounding that even the viceroy watched the situation closely, and gave orders for the improvement of the main road.

One would not expect any notable standard of highway building, and in fact it was not needed. The improvement of the road apparently involved the conscription of some local Indians, who with hand tools eased the grades at the stream crossings and steeper ravines, rolled boulders away in the passes, and perhaps made a dugway here and there around a hillside. Bridges were still a non-essential luxury. Even so close to Mexico City as San Juan del Río there was no bridge for at least a decade after Tolosa's discovery. When the water was high there, the teamsters merely had to wait, though they might wait for a week.

Still, the traffic moved. To the Chichimecas looking out from their rocky hillsides it must have seemed an invasion. There were the Spaniards, on horseback and on foot, eager-faced and hurrying up to the mines. Then there were the long strings of *tamenes,* the Indian bearers, who in these early Spanish times were still doing the work which they had done before the introduction of domestic animals — and their descendants have by no means entirely left off doing such work even now (see Picture 36).

Then, before long, the carts began to pass, strange in themselves, to Chichimecas, and drawn by strange animals. (The ox-carts doubtless looked about the same as those you see, even now, anywhere south of Mexico City. See Picture 60.) Finally, in a few years, after the roads had been improved, the Chichimecas began to see wagons, drawn by two or three or four teams of mules.

There must have been many interesting incidents during the time of opening the highway, and some small record is preserved. There was, for instance, a famous character named Sebastián de Aparicio. Both he and another man, Martin Enríquez, are put forward as the first to take wagons through to Zacatecas. The curious thing about the former, however, is that he was a friar, and took up managing wagon-trains as an extra-curricular activity.

This, then, was the general situation between Mexico City and Zacatecas for a considerable time (a whole generation, it would seem) after the discovery. The main road went northwest through Querétero, and then through the little settlement called San Miguel (which now has added the distinguishing term, Allende), and then on across barren uplands, where now no important road penetrates. Other roads ran northward from Jalisco and Michoacan, and some of these followed much of the line of the present highway. Sometime, moreover, a route was opened up from Querétaro westward into the Bajío to connect with the road from Michoacan, and thus establish the full line of Mexico 45 as far as Zacatecas.

Gradually this secondary route became more important. The original main road had the advantage of crossing uplands and not being subject to floods, and also it was shorter. But the road through the Bajío was flatter and smoother, and passed through rich country, so that ranches and little settlements began to be located along it. In addition, it had its own rich silver strike at Guanajuato. Finally, and this was very important, it merely passed through the edge of the Chichimeca country, and therefore was safer.

As was only to be expected, hostilities had soon broken out. The tribesmen must have been angered at the invasion of their territory and at the enslavement of some of them for work in the mines, and also they saw the chance for plunder. Doubtless there were clashes very early. By 1552 the Chichimecas were ravaging the country even well south of Querétaro. A great war-chief arose, named Maxorro. Probably under his leadership, the Chichimecas attacked a train of sixty wagons in 1554 at Ojuelos Pass, about half way on the main road between Querétaro and Zacatecas. Only one wagon managed to escape.

The Spaniards tried to meet the threat by building and garrisoning little forts, spaced along the highway. This helped, but raids and ambushes still continued, and even the road through the Bajío was far from safe. So presidios or defended towns were established along it at Celaya, León, San Juan de Lagos, and Aguas calientes. In addition troops were stationed at Guanajuato, only a few miles off the highway.

Celaya was founded shortly after 1570; León, in 1576. After this time the road through the Bajío must have rapidly become the more important one. The original main road, badly exposed to attack, lapsed into disuse. Thus the wild Chichimecas contributed to fixing the route of a modern highway.

In the meantime, however, much had been happening in the North. Silver and souls still lured the Spaniards on.

First went the explorers, making what were called *entradas,* "entrances." On horseback, usually with at least one hardy friar accompanying them, the captains and their men wandered widely. But mere exploration does not determine a road, and so is not part of this story. A fixed line of communication was established only as a new more northerly settlement was founded and the road was pushed forward. It went on northward in four jumps.

The first of these took the road another hundred miles, from Zacatecas to the Sombrerete area, where silver mines were opened about 1557. Then, with the foundation of Durango in 1563, came the second jump, of 75 miles more. This city, however, was not founded because of a silver-strike, but because it lay in a rich valley and could produce cattle and corn to supply the mining towns.

The third jump of more than two hundred miles, was to the Parral district, where mines were discovered in the middle 1560's. Parral is more than two hundred miles north of Durango.

Exploration and settlement in all this middle region of the North are largely connected with the boy-wonder among the *conquistadores,* Francisco de Ibarra. He led his first *entrada* at the age of sixteen, and he was almost constantly in the saddle until he retired from exploring as a worn-out veteran at the age of twenty-seven. He it was who founded Durango, naming it for the native city of his family in the Basque country of Spain. This name and others should make us remember the strong Basque element among the Spaniards who thus advanced northwards. Others of their names are Celaya, El Bajío, and La Bufa.

When they had reached the Parral district, the Spaniards had really penetrated all the way through the Chichimeca country, and had come to a region in which many of the tribes, though scarcely rating as civilized, at least practiced agriculture, and lived in the settled villages which the Spaniards called *pueblos.* In the 1580's some Spanish expeditions pressed on northward, and reached the region which has eventually come to be known as New Mexico. These expeditions need not be of concern to us, because they traveled only by horseback or on foot, and also because they departed a long way from the route which the highway was later to follow. The actual establishment of the road had to wait some years for one who was a greater even than Francisco de Ibarra, and as the leader of a people across a wilderness might almost be compared to Moses himself. He may even be said in some ways to outrate Moses, for he traversed a much greater distance than from Egypt to Moab, and he took only something more than forty days, not forty years, for the journey.

This leader was Don Juan de Oñate. He himself came of a prominent and wealthy Spanish family, one which had already contributed largely to the conquest of the North. His wife was a granddaughter of Cortez and a great-granddaughter of Montezuma. Oñate was given a royal grant to occupy the northern region, vaguely known as New Mexico. From such a large area there would be good chances of finding silver mines, and in any case it contained towns of industrious Indians and was worth occupying.

Oñate, using his own great wealth, recruited soldiers and colonists around Mexico City and Zacatecas, and bought animals and supplies. Then, late in 1597, he advanced north as far as Parral and a little beyond. There, on some stream called San Gerónimo, a muster was held, which might be compared to Moses's numbering of the Israelites. Also, in the thorough-going Spanish manner of those times, an inventory of supplies was taken, and written down, and sent back for safe keeping. The whole company consisted of about four hundred men, and 130 of these had their families with them. The livestock totaled seven thousand head. Oñate's own property was most carefully listed. He was credited with 846 goats, 198 oxen, 2517 sheep and lambs, 383 rams, 119 horses, 101 mares, 96 colts, 41 mules and burros, and finally 53 hogs — "large and small, boars and sows, two of them lame."

There was necessarily a tremendous burden of food and supplies, including horseshoes, plowshares, shields, lances, arquebuses, armor, some small cannon, iron and steel to be worked up, paper, wine, oil, medicines, clothing, and the usual assortment of beads, combs, mirrors, needles, and hawk's bells to trade to the Indians. But — what is most interesting in connection with the history of the road — these supplies were carried, not on the backs of Indians or by burros or pack-mules, but in wheeled vehicles. These totaled 83 — wagons, carts, and two coaches.

Besides Oñate, we should also record the name Vicente de Zaldívar. He ranked as sergeant-major, and "chief officer of the entire army." His principal service was as a scout, and he pioneered several hundred miles of the modern highway. That he may not remain too shadowy a figure, let it be known that the muster-role listed him as being a native of Zacatecas, well-built, twenty-eight years of age, having a chestnut-colored beard.

So, on January 26, the great expedition pushed off northward. This was the middle of the dry season, and the dust must have risen up like a pillar of cloud by day from the trampling feet of all the animals, and the passing of the long wagon train, and from the trudging of all the people who walked beside the wagons. No one has left any description of how they marched, but we know that the chestnut-bearded sergeant rode far ahead, with his scouts. Also we can at least imagine the mounted men spread out on the flanks for patrols, and the flocks and herds driven onward, somewhere within the line of the patrols, and at the center the mile-long wagon-train, thin and winding like a snake, dipping to the hollows and lifting to the rises, twisting to right and left to follow the lay of the land, forever working north-ward. Also, you must not forget Don Juan himself, riding here or there, praising or reprimanding, ordering and directing, heavy with the weight of responsibility, yet his eyes alit with the fiery light that blazes in the glance of a *conquistador*.

His was a bold adventure — to move so many people, including women and children, so far across country that had never before been traversed by wheeled vehicles, if, indeed, traversed at all. The very size of the expedi-tion, however, was to its advantage in some ways. To break a road in is no more difficult for 83 wagons than for one wagon, but the larger expedition supplies more workmen. Doubtless just as there were soldiers and team-sters, so there was a regular road-working detail. The problem cannot have been too great, for in the dry season the streams were low and the ground was generally firm. In that open plateau country the mountains separating valley from valley are low and not unduly rough.

As to where they went, we know a little from the itinerary — "prepared by a witness, a priest, who saw and experienced it all and who reports the truth." In his words, "We went north-northwest one-fourth degree, which direction we tried to follow whenever we could." Such a route — call it a little west of north — would take them through country to the west of the present highway, until they reached a point forty miles south of Chihuahua. The earlier expeditions to New Mexico had followed the Conchos River, as the highway now does for many miles. Oñate, however, avoided this route, probably because it was longer and also because he had heard from earlier explorers that the Conchos, lower down, passed through a canyon too diffi-cult for wagons.

Such a numerous and miscellaneous and heavily laden party was not to be pushed too hard. Five days' march took them to a crossing of the upper Conchos River, perhaps not far from where that stream reaches its southern-most point and starts to flow northwest. There they halted a week. Then with two days' march, a day's rest, and another day's march they came to the San Pedro River on February 10.

Again their journeyings and encampings make one think of the Children of Israel, and most likely the priest, when he made his entries in the log-book, thought also of *Numbers*, 21:

> From thence they removed, and pitched in the valley of Zared.
> From thence they removed, and pitched on the other side of Arnon, which is in the wilderness. . . .
> And from thence they went to Beer: that is the well whereof the Lord spake unto Moses, Gather the people together, and I will give them water.

Water — enough of it for four hundred people and seven thousand animals — must, indeed, have been the chief problem. Even if the expedition moved in two sections, the need of either section would have exhausted an ordinary desert spring, long before the last thirsty sheep could have got anywhere near it. Even so, Oñate chose to march in the dry season, probably fearing the mud and swollen streams of the summer months. Also, he may not have realized that the farther north he went, the drier the country would get. Many stretches are almost pure desert, and even now on a hot day can be terrifying to a tourist who is unused to arid sands. The monotonous repetition of place names is enough to indicate the way in which water determines everything in that country — Ojo and Ojito (spring), Agua (water), Pozo (well) Charco (pool) and Alamos and Sauces for the cottonwoods and scrubby willows that grow near water.

On the San Pedro River, where there was water and pasturage, Oñate halted for a month, partly to give a lagging party of friars a chance to catch up, but also to send a scouting party northward — to find a route passable for wagons, and to discover watering-places.

Zaldívar, the chestnut-bearded sergeant, went ahead with seventeen mounted men.

As he himself reported later:

> We traveled many days and suffered intolerable hardships from hunger and thirst, even going without water for two or three days at a time and many of our horses becoming exhausted . . . we were compelled to kill horses for food . . . when we were marching through rugged country . . . the Indians met us hostilely and tried to stop us . . . I often endangered my own life and encouraged my companions to do like-

wise . . . I went ahead until I succeeded in finding a way with watering-places.

Zaldívar got back to camp early on the morning of February 10. Oñate must have been waiting impatiently, for on that very day the expedition moved ahead, and made a march of ten miles.

Still, they continued to move slowly. There was plenty of time, and it was the long pull that counted. Usually they marched two or three days and then halted for a day, or perhaps longer. From one of these camps Zaldívar was again sent ahead, with five men. This time he was able to make friends with the Indians:

> I obtained guides and discovered the Rio del Norte [Rio Grande] and
> a good road with adequate water . . . and I did not lose a single man.

Behind him, not waiting for his return this time, the people and wagons and flocks and herds came toiling on. (By this time we can hope that the Governor's two lame hogs had either got well or been barbecued.) April 1 started out to be a bad day, as they entered on a dry drive of twenty-five miles. But, though it was early in the season for rain, there was a heavy shower — as we should say, by good luck. Perhaps, however the priest remembered how the congregation murmured in the desert of Zin and how the Lord worked a miracle to bring water from the rock so that the people drank "and their beasts also." So he wrote simply:

> God aided us with a downpour so heavy that great pools were formed.
> Then we unyoked the cattle, and more than five thousand head . . .
> drank, and later two thousand more . . . that were following behind. So
> we named this place Help of Heaven.

By this time they were north of Chihuahua and following the line of the highway. Shortly afterwards Zaldívar must have been back with his news of the passable route. The shower had actually solved most of the problems for the time being, by filling the pools.

On April 12 the expedition arrived at the sand-dunes, through which the highway passes, about twenty-five miles south of the Rio Grande. Here they halted for five days. Because there was not enough water, the live-stock had to be driven across eastward to another point on the river to be watered and pastured. Just how it was all done we cannot be sure, but on April 19 a sufficient number of oxen had been brought back so that half the wagons could begin the passage of the dunes. This detachment traveled ten miles, which should have taken them through the actual dunes. They made a dry camp, and on the next day reached the river. The rest of the wagons soon followed.

A few days later the now united expedition had shifted camp a few miles upstream to where the scouts had found a ford, so that the Spaniards called that place El Paso, "the crossing." (It is a few miles south of the city now so named.) There, on April 30, 1598, Don Juan de Oñate, with most elaborate ceremonies, took formal possession of "all the kingdoms and provinces of New Mexico." In the lengthy document recording these acts he saw fit to include some references not uncomplimentary to himself, but since he had just successfully completed a perilous four-hundred mile journey and does not depart from fact, we can scarcely consider him boast-ful. He recorded, for instance, that he had come through with "wagons, carts, carriages," and that he had arrived at the Rio Grande with more people than he had led out, because — as he goes on to put it, with a high regard for morality — he had brought many married people with him. Also, he stated that he had opened, across nearly a hundred leagues of unin-habited country, "a road for carts, broad and level . . . so that it may be traveled without difficulty."

(And the rest of the acts of Oñate, how he journeyed, and how he ruled, behold, they are written in the books of the chronicles of New Mexico.)

Thus, in 1598, nine years before the landing at Jamestown, it was finished. There was a road for wheeled vehicles all the way from Mexico City to El Paso.

At this point the story of the King's Road of the Interior might be dropped, but some of its later vicissitudes may be pleasantly recorded.

Throughout most of the seventeenth century the most remarkable traffic using this route consisted of the wagon-trains which passed between Mexico City and the missions of New Mexico, making a round-trip once every three years. At least, once every three years was the schedule, but sometimes the interval stretched out to four years, and even more. As with Oñate's expedition, we know little about what these caravans actually looked like, what was their manner of march, and what were their individual adventures. But from the carefully kept records we know a great deal about their equipment and their cargoes. The inventory of the wagon-train of 1631 runs through twelve pages of small print. The first item (very properly) is 45 gallons of sacramental wine. Then follows, carefully itemized, a list of practically everything you can imagine — food, clothing, writing materials, kitchen-utensils, medicines, tools, church-supplies. Among the last is doubtless to be included an oil painting, presumably of a saint, "two and a half yards in height, with gilded frame." Included also were spices (saffron, pepper, cinnamon), along with cheese, wine (not sacramental), and oysters (presumably, dried). The use of certain objects was specified — "one leg for the base of the altar," "one large latch for the church door," "four dozen hens for those may be sick during the journey," and with a delightful specificity, "a hat, for a Spanish lay brother named Diego Gómez."

The thirty-two wagons were divided into two sections, and each of these into two sub-sections. Each wagon was drawn by eight mules, and each mule of each leading wagon of the two main sections was to wear a bell.

Not only were there to be thirty-two spare mules, but also spare parts of all kinds — axles, spokes, mule-shoes. Most interesting is the assignment to each wagon of what means literally in Spanish "half an Indian woman." Doubtless this means that there was an Indian woman (duties unspecified) for every two wagons.

Yes, there was traffic on the road even in the seventeenth century, and after the discovery of the rich silver mines near Chihuahua, soon after 1700, there must have been more traffic as far as that locality.

During the eighteenth century, however, Spain and all her colonies were sinking into a languor of decadence, and many of the silver mines were playing out. In fact, during this time one has difficulty in finding out about the road at all. There seem to be no colorful accounts left by travelers who went over it. For 1766, indeed, we have the record left by de la Fora, but his are only the summary and matter-of-fact notes of an engineer, and they tell us little except that the road was still open and seems to have followed the same route, approximately, as it does now. The stone bridge at San Juan del Río was standing (doubtless the same one that is there now), but there was no bridge across the river at Lagos. A somber note, reminiscent of those early days of the Chichimeca hostilities creeps into this narrative when he records that the people around Chihuahua were perishing because of Indian attacks.

With the nineteenth century came wars and disturbances — first the revolt againt Spain and then revolutions in rapid succession. Bridges were destroyed in the wars, or merely fell into decay. Summer cloudbursts left gullies across the road, and no one repaired them. Mine after mine was closing down. All the while, the Indians were pressing in for plunder and scalps — Apaches from the northwest, Comanches from the northeast.

Any untended road in a country of heavy showers deteriorates rapidly as the ruts left by the wagon-wheels become channels for running water. In that open plateau country the teamsters could often merely shift ground and start a new track somewhere else, but much of the road seems to have become almost impassable for wagons.

The famous Alexander von Humboldt, who was in Mexico during 1803, noted that "thousands of mules" arrived weekly in Mexico City from Chihuahua and Durango bringing silver, hides, tallow, wine, and flour. They returned with woolen cloth of Puebla and Querétaro, iron, steel, and mercury, and manufactured goods from Europe and the Philippine Islands. He wrote also, "In the present bad state of the roads, wagons are not established for the conveyance of goods." Carriages, however, took passengers to the north, but we cannot envy those passengers the jolting they must have had from such a road.

We are fortunate in having three vivid accounts of travel over the road in the second quarter of the nineteenth century. On November 3, 1826, Sir Henry Ward, British chargé d'affaires in Mexico, set out on a journey northward to look at mining properties and see the country. The manner in which he traveled and the vigor with which he pressed on to make little of obstacles help us understand why the British dominated the world in that century. Ward was accompanied by four gentlemen, his family, and a retinue of servants. The family consisted of Mrs. Ward and two children — one of them a baby only five months old! A large coach, drawn by eight mules, was provided for the women and children, but Mrs. Ward preferred riding horseback to being jostled on wheels, and usually left the coach to her two Mexican maids and the children. There were also a footman, a

coachman, a "lad," two mule-drivers, two horse-wranglers, and some miscellaneous servants. Altogether they set out with sixteen men, well mounted
and armed, eight baggage mules, eight loose horses, and a number of dogs.
Mrs. Ward, who served as the artist for the expedition, has left us a picture
of the coach, and thus we know that there was also a parrot in a cage,
swung beneath. The coach was generally festooned with strips of dried
beef, and handkerchiefs full of onions and tortillas, tied there by the
servants.

The party was strong enough to escape trouble from bandits, though
many sections were considered dangerous. As for the road itself, Ward
noted it most often as execrable. Apparently it had reverted to an almost
natural state, being extremely bad where the country was rough, but good
in the places where the country was open and the soil firm. Near Zacatecas
a certain descent was covered with fragments of rock, and almost impassable for carriages or horsemen. But between Aguascalientes and Zacatecas there was a steady traffic of large wagons, mostly laden with chiles,
drawn each by six oxen, and north of Zacatecas the road won the rating
"excellent" over a stretch of forty miles.

Ward went only as far as Durango, but another traveler has left good
descriptions of the northern part of the road for the year 1835. This was
Josiah Gregg, the American author of the famous *Commerce of the Prairies*.
By the time he arrived in El Paso, he had already journeyed all the way
from Missouri, and so was an experienced traveler in the wilderness. Therefore, his standards of what constitute a good road must have become
extremely low. Nevertheless, it is interesting to note that he had no difficulty in taking wagons all the way to Aguascalientes and back. This whole
northern country is so easy to traverse that by Gregg's time a number of
alternate routes had been developed, and a traveler could pick whichever
one seemed most advantageous at the time, according to the weather, or
the threat of Indian attack, or his desire to keep away from the nosy officials of the towns. Gregg, traveling in the dry season, marveled at the
excellence of these natural roads: "Some of these table-plain highways,
though of but a dry sandy and clayey soil, are as firm as a brick pavement.
In some places, for miles, I have remarked that the nail-heads of my shod
animals would hardly leave any visible impression." Gregg's troubles were
not with the road, but he had his worries about Indians and bandits, and

had to circumvent petty officials, and to keep out of the way of a Federal army advancing to quell a revolution at Zacatecas.

But of all who ever traveled the road, none can outdo George Augustus Frederick Ruxton, either for being a colorful character, or for having colorful adventures, or for leaving a colorful account. Ruxton, former officer in Her Majesty's 89th Regiment of Foot, soldier of fortune in Spain, adventurer in Africa, hunter in the Canadian wilds, was still only twenty-five years old in 1846. On September 14 of that year, he set out on horseback from Mexico City for the north. Accompanied by a single servant, he planned to make a journey which was considered so hazardous, even in a large party, as to be almost suicidal.

By this time the situation in Mexico, to use a military euphemism, "had deteriorated badly." Banditry was rife; even the towns were lawless. Everywhere north of Zacatecas the Comanches and Apaches were terrorizing the country. United States troops had already invaded Mexico and captured Monterrey. Only a daredevil like Ruxton would have tried it, and even he — we cannot but think — got through more by good luck than by his own skill and courage. He killed a man in a street-fight at León, was shot at from behind by his own servant, had several hairbreadth escapes from Indians.

In general, Ruxton followed the route of the highway, though he left it for some detours. Apparently the road was not much different from what it had been in Ward's time, although possibly it was even a little worse. Only six miles from Mexico City — it was the rainy season — Ruxton found the *camino real* a gigantic mud-hole. A carriage "full of ladies" was stuck in the middle of a puddle, with its mules unharnessed and grazing by the roadside, and the men away seeking assistance. Even some charcoal-laden donkeys were mired down. There seems to have been the same alternation of almost impassable stretches and good natural roadway which was notable in Ward's time. On the "vast plains" of the Bajío, Ruxton met no other travelers than the *arrieros* with their pack trains of mules. In the rough country beyond León, where the highway still crosses a range of hills, he noted the mule-path as "rough and dangerous." But near Fresnillo he met a wagon bearing bars of silver to the mint at Zacatecas. Since it was drawn by six mules, "galloping at their utmost speed," the road here must have been excellent.

North of Durango, the natural road still remained as Gregg had described it, and the Indians, not the road, were the hazard. On his third day out of Durango, Ruxton encountered a train of nearly forty wagons which had come all the way from Missouri.

Farther north Ruxton met still more vicissitudes. They can best be read in his own famous book, *Adventures in Mexico and the Rocky Mountains.*

Our Mexican war supplied one interesting bit of highway history — the march of Doniphan's column. His men were mostly from the backwoods and the frontier and formed a very informal military organization, the First Missouri Mounted Volunteers. Some historians state that the march of Doniphan's men is the longest recorded in history, but I think that other claims can be entered — for instance, that of the First Macedonian Armored under the command of Alexander Philipson.

When they got to El Paso, the men of the First Missouri had already marched all the way from their home state. As Doniphan advanced on Chihuahua, the souls of Oñate and Zaldívar must have stirred restlessly. Here was a northern heretic invading their own country by means of the road that they themselves had opened up. (So we might feel, if the Russians should some day invade us by means of the Alaska Highway.)

Doniphan came on across the desert. Beside his seven hundred Missourians he had some artillerymen with six guns. In addition there were three hundred traders and teamsters, organized to fight, and bringing along a tremendous train of four hundred wagons.

The Mexicans collected a much larger force, though it was poorly armed and hardly trained at all. Their military engineer erected strong fortifications at a well-chosen spot, where the road crossed the small Sacramento River, about twenty miles north of Chihuahua. By the rules, Doniphan should then have retreated across the desert. He faced a bad situation. The Mexican position was too strong to take by direct attack; if he tried a flanking movement across country, he would have to leave his wagon-train exposed to the numerous Mexican cavalry. At least, that was what any European military expert would have said — not knowing American mule-skinners who had brought wagons over the Santa Fe Trail.

Doniphan merely did what Oñate had done — took his wagons across country. Thus the little battle of the Sacramento became something perhaps unique in that its deciding maneuver was a flanking movement of the wagon-train. Once the whole force, wagons and all, had come around on the Mexican left, the guns opened up on the now very nervous defenders of the outflanked redoubts. Then the Missourians charged—and next day occupied Chihuahua.

Later, Doniphan's little army marched on southward — accompanied by a certain number of Chihuahua *señoritas,* who had put on pants and decided to follow their soldier-boys. (We've already written, haven't we, that the First Missouri was a highly informal outfit?) In this march to join other American forces at Saltillo, the column followed the line of the highway clear to Jiménez — the farthest that any American troops ever reached in this part of Mexico, except for a few of Pershing's troopers who got to the outskirts of Parral while hunting Villa in 1916.

Generally speaking, no one wants to say a good word for our Mexican War these days, but in reality it may be claimed the best thing that ever happened for all this northern country. Once the Americans were established on the Rio Grande and in Arizona, they soon wiped out the Comanches and got the Apaches under some kind of control. Then, at last, a man's scalp became moderately safe in the states of Chihuahua and Durango. Otherwise, as things had been going for a hundred years, the Indians might well have wiped out the Mexicans north of Zacatecas.

In the latter part of the nineteenth century there is little to tell of the road. This was the railroad era, in Mexico, as elsewhere. Once the rails had been laid from El Paso to Mexico City, the old highway, after an active life of about three centuries, lapsed into disuse. Moreover, the railroad era in Mexico lasted at least thirty years longer than in the United States. For instance, the campaigning of Pancho Villa around Chihuahua was based upon the railroads. Most people think of Villa as a dashing leader of the bandit-like horsemen, but in reality he liked to transport his troops by railway, and most of his men were more used to riding freight cars than to riding horses.

Only after 1940 was appreciable progress made at opening up the old highway for automobile traffic. Then, like most highways, it was built as a city-to-city road. Thus it still goes around to touch Camargo and Jiménez and then bends sharply back to Parral, increasing its total length considerably. By 1948 the road was in fairly good condition, but paving was not completed until 1950.

I write from experience. My wife and I headed south in March, 1949. I had been informed by a friend, who had driven that way the year before, that the road was in excellent condition; what he had not considered was that it would be in bad condition, once paving-operations started.

Everything was fine as far as Parral, and there we filled the gas-tank. A few miles beyond, the pavement ended, and since work was in progress, we were shunted off on many long and rough and dusty detours. For a while everything went pleasantly enough, in spite of the detours. At the Nazas River there was a little hand-operated ferry, and the ferrymen called for music. We got something on the radio, and went across in fine style.

Beyond that, things began to get tough. We could buy no gasoline in any of the villages, and the indicator-needle swung over to E. Darkness came. We drove on, through detours with dust six inches deep, not knowing where we were half the time, expecting any moment to have the engine cough and die.

We blundered into a little village, pretty well convinced that we would have to sleep there in the car that night, since our gasoline was too low, and we could not keep ourselves on the road anyway. But we found there an itinerant peddler of patent-medicines in an old station wagon. He had a can of gas, and kindly sold us two gallons. We got directions from him how to go, and wandered on again in the darkness, trusting that two gallons would take us to Durango. Within a mile the road was blocked again, and we were shunted off into a twisting and dusty trail. It took us to another village, where only one light was burning. I went to that house to try, this time, to pick up somebody whom we could take along as a guide. The man who stepped up to talk to me was wearing a pistol three feet long. (My wife thinks it may have lacked a few inches of being three feet, but I state the way it looked to me.) Instead of taking our money from us, however, this mustachioed artilleryman said to me, as well as I could understand his Spanish — that we did not need a guide, but could follow behind another car that was going our way. In this car were four Mexicans with handkerchiefs tied round the lower parts of their faces. Having seen plenty of people like that in Westerns, I knew that these were bandits. But since the man with the pistol told us to follow them, I thought that I might as well be robbed in the desert as robbed in the village, and I followed. There were many little side-trails branching off, and I had to keep close in the dust of the other car to see the tail-light at all. I kept hoping that the four bandits would be chivalrous enough merely to take our money and not to shoot us.

After a while the other car stopped, and one of the men came walking back. "Well," I thought, "this is it!"

But he merely explained in broken English that they had had to stop because the car was boiling, and that from here on we could proceed without danger of being lost. At this point I decided that they were, quite sensibly, wearing the handkerchiefs to keep dust out of their nostrils.

So we went on, and about midnight came around a hill and saw the lights of Durango.

Since then I have twice driven that same stretch in the daylight. It is now all paved, and I have been unable to recognize any single point by which I passed on that night. There are two or three villages a little off the highway, which must include the ones where I encountered the snake-oil vendor and the artilleryman. Incidentally, it has been my experience in Mexico that even rough-looking characters with pistols are likely to be courteous and helpful to a tourist.

In 1950 the completed highway leaped into the sporting headlines all over the world as the line of the great Mexican road race. Oldsmobiles, Hudsons, Fords, Jaguars, Alfa Romeos and the rest of the 132 entries, went barreling through at two miles a minute, where the chestnut-bearded sergeant had explored the way for Oñate's ox-carts, and where young Francisco de Ibarra had led his horsemen, and where the Indian burden-bearers had toiled northward to the mines of Zacatecas more than four hundred years earlier.

① Sand Dunes

✛ [1]To the tourist entering from the United States, Mexico fails to present, by far, her fairest aspect. After the irrigated districts around Ciudad Juárez, the highway passes through country which becomes more and more desert-like until the ultimate is reached in Los Médanos, the Sand Dunes. These begin a little to the south of the small settlement of Samalayuca, and extend for several miles, even though the highway crosses them at their narrowest point. From the rises the white wave-like dunes stretch off for many miles to east and west.

The picture is taken at Kilometer 2063, looking south. The bus, accom-

[1]A plus sign indicates that in the picture the direction of the view of the highway is away from the United States; a minus sign indicates the opposite.

panied by its dark patch of shadow from a high morning sun, is headed toward Chihuahua, away from the observer, though for some reason most people seem first to see it as approaching on the wrong side of the highway.

The road here runs close to the railroad with its two pole-lines; the closer of these, with its tall metal poles and short cross-bars, is typically Mexican.

Although the dunes in many parts display an unbroken expanse of whiteness, in this particular spot the surface is broken and the movement of sand by the wind is somewhat impeded by the growth of hardy desert plants. Each plant anchors the sand around it, and the whole situation can be described as a battle, throughout the centuries, between plants and wind, with the sand passive between them. The plants are conservative; the wind, destructive. The plants try to hold what they have gained, and in good years to extend themselves. The wind tries either to bury the plants, or to blow the sand away from their roots. To the left of the road, in the distance, a crest of sand seems to be advancing upon some doomed plants before it. Closer at hand, some clumps grow at the top of hummocks, which the wind is threatening to blow out from beneath. These dunes represent the bed of a long dry lake, probably its retreating shoreline of beaches. The last remnant of what must have been a large body of water is to be seen some thirty miles to the south as the Laguna de Patos, "Duck Lake."

Oñate's expedition crossed this narrow neck of the dunes in 1598 (see page 49), and it was the route of passage for light traffic in later years. Heavy wagons generally detoured by a much longer route, which brought them to the Rio Grande some thirty-five miles below El Paso.

2 Chihuahua

● Being only a short day's drive south of the border, Chihuahua displays many of the traits of a "North-American" city, such as a parking problem, overhead wires, and men with briefcases.

From here, where the highway crosses the northern side of the central plaza, the view is southwest on an August morning (10.30 by the cathedral clock), with the thunderclouds for the afternoon shower building up in the distance. The summer days are hot, particularly in the mornings, before the clouds shut off the sun, so that even in the center of the city, men walk coatless, in sport-shirts, as in the cities of our own South.

But Chihuahua, Americanized though it is, shows the contrast of old and new that is so typical of much of Mexico. Here the parked automobiles contrast with the bony old horse pulling a wagon, and the wagon itself is constructed from an old automobile chassis, with automobile-wheels on the rear and cart-wheels on the front.

The plaza is typically Mexican, or "Old-Mexican." Cast-iron benches, mostly empty now in the heat of the day, surround it. Also of elaborate ironwork is the inevitable bandstand, here seen at the right.

Beyond the plaza stand some of the solid but ornate buildings usually to be ascribed to the Díaz era, before the outbreak of the Revolution in 1910.

Dominating everything is the cathedral, begun in 1717 and finished in 1789, a notable example of Mexican baroque, rising in a rhythm of threes, in the comparatively simple style erected before the Churrigueresque began to dominate after 1750. It is dedicated to St. Francis, who with the apostles stands as one of the thirteen statues in the niches of the façade. The firmly based but aspiring towers rise to 146 feet, massive but elegant. Their fine proportions even yet testify to the munificent contributions supplied by the wealth of the near-by Santa Eulalia silver mines, and to the vigor of the architectural tradition, even in this far-off corner of New Spain.

The clock covers the spot where the royal arms were originally carved. In 1847 Ruxton (see page 54) saw 170 Apache scalps displayed as trophies over the main portal.

 **3** After The Shower

✛ As in most of the western United States, water "determines" in northern Mexico. Much of the state of Chihuahua has about 15 inches of rainfall a year, mostly concentrated in the summer. A semi-desert climate results, and water is all the more appreciated when it is available.

On this August day the storm has come early and has been severe, so that at 1.30 the rain has ceased, and the children in the village, and a few mothers, have hurried out to wade in the run-off which courses along between the houses and the highway like a small flood. People of a little unattractive village like this one are not used to having tourists stop, and so there is much interest in the photographer, and no attempt at soliciting money.

There is nothing typically Mexican in any of the clothes that the people here are wearing. They are merely cheap factory-made products, bought across the counter, not differing in style (if such a word can be used) from such clothing seen in the United States.

The village itself is only in part typical of Mexico, being really a factory town associated with a near-by smelter. It is, moreover, rather recent, as is evidenced by the structures being set far back from the highway, thus indicative of construction after the highway itself. The buildings themselves, however, are what one can expect in all of northern Mexico — flat-roofed, low, box-like adobes. As is customary, they bear signs advertising cigarettes, beer, and soft drinks.

The highway, still slick from the recent rain, leads straight ahead toward the distant peak, but will swing toward the right before approaching it. The only vehicle in sight is a truck, as may be expected in most of Mexico, for away from the cities trucks and buses far outnumber private cars.

The three-wire high-tension power-line at the left does not follow the road for long, and is more suggestive of the United States than of Mexico. Other wires are conspicuously absent, since they follow the railway.

 Tangent

✚ Straightaways — "tangents," in the language of road-engineers — are common in northern Mexico. Here the point of view is from a slight rise about twenty miles from Jiménez, looking toward Parral, which lies among the distant hills some twenty-five miles away. Several miles of straight road are in view. It is all empty except for a single truck, about a mile away, so nearly in the center of the road that one hesitates to say whether it is approaching or departing.

Such a straightaway invites fast driving, but the absence of fences should be noted. Even such a semi-desert region as this is good-enough pasture-land, and cattle and burros are likely to come strolling across the road. In open country they can be seen a long way off, but care should be exercised, even so.

This is a typical-enough landscape of northern Mexico along the highway — a broad, semi-desert valley, bounded by low treeless mountains, producing a fine effect of open space. In the middle distance, a little beyond the truck on the road, the highway crosses a stream course, and this is marked by a dark line of tree-growth. There are actually a few fields of cotton and some block-like adobe houses to the left of the highway near the stream, but these are hardly to be seen in the picture.

The magnificent domination of the clouds is to be expected of the Mexican plateau in the summer. A shower is already falling upon the distant mountains to the right. The picture was taken about 5.30 in the afternoon. A little while later we entered the storm-area ahead, and we came into Parral through a tremendous downpour, with thunder and lightning, to find the town half-flooded.

❺ Church and Village

✚ This is Rodeo, a name indicating originally a place where a round-up was held, not a circus-like celebration. This small and poor village about 120 miles north of Durango stands upon stony and arid ground, as the foreground of the picture, with its pebble-strewn earth and thin growth of mesquite, amply demonstrates. The Nazas River, however, is only about a mile away, to the left, and cornfields are strung along its bottom-lands.

The opening of the highway has brought a gas-station and restaurant. Before that time there was neither road nor railroad, and the villagers must have lived, as they had been living for probably three centuries, essentially as a self-contained unit. Even yet, they live chiefly by subsistent farming, and life is at a primitive level.

Here seen against the sun from a point half a mile to the north, the village is dominated by its great church, standing on the highest point. Pink in color, conspicuously in view for several miles along the highway, the church is of no great distinction architecturally, and is here seen at its worst, from the side, so that it seems to have only one tower. It is, however, typical of Mexican churches, consisting of a cross-shaped box-like structure, set off by towers flanking the main portal, and by a dome over the crossing. It is also symbolically typical in its domination of the village. Actually, it is a great deal larger than practical need would warrant, thus also indicating the domination of the Church in early Mexican history, particularly in communities largely Indian.

The village itself, only partially in view, is well enough suggested by the dark masses of the block-like adobe structures extending to the left from the gas-station.

Historically, Rodeo must have grown up as a village on the King's Road of the Interior, which was pushed northward to the silver mines of the Parral district, probably along this route, in the fifteen-sixties. During the Chichimeca wars of the later sixteenth century, the Tepehuanes of this region sometimes favored the Chichimecas and sometimes kept neutral. They were later pacified, partly by arms and partly by gifts of food and clothing and the missionary work of the friars. But Spanish rule must have lain heavily upon them, for in 1616 they rose in revolt, only to be "pacified" again. The inhabitants of the present village, almost pure Indian in blood, are doubtless the descendants of the Tepehuanes, although they may be mingled with the more southern Indians whom the Spaniards brought northward in large numbers as laborers.

As so often on the plateau during the summer, the clouds form the most magnificent part of the landscape, dwarfing the distant mountains, and silhouetting the heavy darkness of the church against their own aspiring brightness.

6 View of the City from the East

● Thus using a title that is reminiscent of a thousand engravings and lithographs in nineteenth-century travel books, we offer what is actually Durango, though it might be, well enough, any other north-Mexican city. Notable are the flat low lines of the buildings in general, broken by the domes and towers of the cathedral and the other churches.

The view is here from the lower slope of the Cerro de Mercado, which bears the name of the Spaniard who first penetrated this area, being lured by tales of a hill which was solid silver. In reality the hill turned out to be iron ore, which is now being worked.

In the foreground, two yuccas, similar to the Joshua trees of California and locally known as "palms," raise their grotesque forms. Two women walk along the path, one of them bearing the customary load of laundry on her head. Beyond the women, near another Joshua tree, two horses graze side by side, not out of friendship, but because their front feet are tied together, Mexican fashion, as a means of hampering their movement and preventing them from straying.

Beyond the horses, to the right, is the baseball field, evidence of the enthusiastic reception which "beisbol" has recently received in Mexico.

Over the top of the Joshua tree to the left, beyond the sidetracked freight cars, rise the twin towers of the cathedral, constructed in the years 1695 to 1750, and showing — as might be expected — a considerable family resemblance to that of Chihuahua. The domed church, to the left of the cathedral, is Santa Ana, also a notable colonial structure.

In contrast to such cities as Zacatecas, Parral, and Chihuahua, which began as mining-centers, Durango shows its agricultural origins by its location in a fertile plain, thus taking its place with Aguascalientes and Celaya and other cities founded upon agriculture.

Beyond the plain, to the west, looms the Sierra Madre Occidental, "western mother range." Although these ridges reach to more than 8000 feet, the plain itself is at 6000, and so there is no sense of domination by mountains. In spite of this barrier, Durango is actually in the Pacific basin, and what water escapes from its valley flows out to the south and then westward. By airline the Pacific Ocean is only a hundred miles to the southwest at this point.

The picture was taken at ten in the morning, but the summer thunderheads are already beginning to build up over the mountains.

7 Tropic of Cancer

— To the north, the road still fails by fifty miles to reach the Arctic Circle. To the south, it is so far from reaching the Equator that the distance cannot be profitably calculated. In the center, however, some twenty miles north of Fresnillo, the road crosses the imaginary line of the Tropic of Cancer, and the Mexican highway authorities, with a considerable sense of imagination, announce this fact by means of a road sign, though no house or other mark of human activity, except the highway, is in evidence.

This is a quite typical stretch of north-Mexican landscape. Since it is the wet season, the foreground shows a growth of grass and low annuals with some wild flowers among them. From such vegetation cattle pick up a living. There is also some cactus, but the predominating vegetation consists of desert scrub, to which the Mexicans give the general name zacatal. Mesquite, familiar enough to Texans, is common, along with ocotillo, a plant of which extends a branch across the road sign. This particular area, pocketed among mountains, has less rainfall than Durango, though that city is only a hundred miles to the northwest. Even the hills, though rising to a considerable height, show nothing but scrubby growth, lacking in pine trees.

This area has, in the past, been subject to much volcanic action, and the rocky and peaked appearance of the hills is probably indicative of such origin.

This was the heart of the Chichimeca country, and typical of it. (See page 39.) One can imagine the warriors watching from the rocky hillsides, for the approach of some wagon-train — then the descent, the sudden attack, and the quick withdrawal to the vastnesses of the hills and rocks. On this region a map of 1613 bears the inscription: *Gens barbara arcu et sagittis contenta quibus venationi indulget.* (A savage tribe, content with bow and arrows, with which it hunts.)

Thomas Gage (see page 93) heard much of the Chichimecas: "They are valiant Indians, and hold the Spaniards hard to it; and have great advantage against them in the rocks and mountains, where they abide and cut off many Spaniards." He added: "I have heard some Spaniards say that they fly and climb up the rocks like goats; and when they draw nigh unto them, then they cry out with a hideous noise shooting their arrows at them, and in an instant are departed and fled unto another rock."

Taken about midday, this picture may be contrasted with the preceding one for its cloud-formation. In this drier region only puff-balls of cumulus have appeared as yet, and there is little likelihood that even by late afternoon they will have managed to coalesce into a mass capable of producing a shower.

⑧ Zacatecas

✛ The southbound traveler suddenly sights Zacatecas when he crosses the more-than-eight-thousand-foot crest just to the north of the city, and sees it spread out in the ravines beneath him — surely one of the most picturesque sights of the continent.

The picture presents a nearer view, emphasizing the stone-arched late-eighteenth-century aqueduct. From Roman times until the invention of steel pipe made the inverted siphon possible, such structures were the approved devices to bring water to any city not located on a river, and without them the very existence of many cities would have been impossible. Notable other examples of such structures may be seen in Mexico, at Chihuahua, Querétaro, and Morelia. To keep the old structure from being shaken down by the rumble of modern heavy traffic, six flying buttresses have recently been erected to strengthen it where the highway passes beneath.

At the farther end of the aqueduct, against the skyline, stands the equestrian statue of General Gonzales Ortega, who commanded a division against the "yanquis" at Buena Vista, and was prominent in the operations against the French and in Mexican politics after the fall of Maximilian.

To the right of the statue the tips of the two cathedral towers show above the line of the aqueduct. Built in the seventeenth century from the proceeds of a tax levied upon all the silver mines of the region, this church was designed and executed in lavish style, and is one of the most notable structures of all colonial Mexico.

In the picture the town itself is largely obscured by the aqueduct and the closer buildings. Through the three arches at the right, however, some impression can be gained of the closely packed houses and narrow streets. Beyond the cathedral, to the left, lies the older part of the town, with its even narrower streets, crowded into the ravines.

In the distance rises the dominating mountain known as La Bufa. Forming the summit is the great outcropping of gray rock which is a notable landmark, and may be seen from the highway many miles to the south. The smaller outcropping to the left is crowned by a weather-observatory. In the saddle lies a church dedicated to the Virgin. An old road, so steep as to be scarcely passable except on foot, ascends the face of the mountain to the shrine. A modern automobile road swings around the mountain to the right and reaches the top from the other side.

On the side of the mountain to the right of the road are the remains of a recent inscription welcoming the president to Zacatecas and reading *Benvenido Sr. Presidente* (Welcome, Mr. President).

The sweeping four-lane approach of the highway should be noted. Though not a large city, and no longer very prosperous, Zacatecas has known greatness in the past, and still maintains a touch of the grand manner. (For some details of the origin of the city, see page 42.)

9 Small-Town Plaza

▬ Encarnación de Díaz, like many other Mexican towns, preserves in its very name the conflict — or the union, if one looks at it that way — of the secular and the religious which has filled so large a part of Mexican history. The "Encarnación" derives from a local cult of the Virgin, and is connected with an image preserved in a near-by town. The "Díaz" was added by act of the legislature of the state in 1876, "to celebrate the triumph of the revolution led by General Porfirio Díaz."

At the left, the highway runs off through the solidly-built, narrow street, northward, toward Aguascalientes. Most of the view is of the plaza, full of life on a Sunday morning — at 10.28 to be exact, as the clock on the church tower makes certain.

The scene presents much that is to be expected in a Mexican plaza — elaborately ornamental lamp-posts, benches of cast-iron and artificial stonework, a dominating church with tall trees in its churchyard. Not so common are the carefully cropped evergreens of the plaza itself.

At the left, along the curb, the benches are exposed to the full sun, and are mostly empty. The crowd, all male except for one old woman in mourning, seeks the shade.

Several men, whose sombreros would indicate that they are just in from some ranch, walk across toward the shade, their own shadows clean-cut beside them in the brilliant sunlight. Most likely they have ridden in on a truck, but their rolling gait suggests horsemen. Quite possibly they really are, since the highway here crosses a corner of the state of Jalisco, which is in many ways the Mexican equivalent of Texas.

The plaza is a busy place on a Sunday morning. Two water-carriers pass heavily by, each with two five-gallon cans suspended from a neck-yoke. The boy with the big wicker basket sells rolls and cakes. In the distance a bootblack offers his services.

Beyond the plaza stands the parish church. Like so many Mexican churches it shows the strong and continuing influence of the baroque tradition, and its twin towers rise in graceful elegance to the elaborate metal crosses at their peaks. High towers are common in northern Mexico, which is not subject to earthquakes.

⑩ Center of Mexico

• On a mountain-top in the state of Guanajuato has been erected the colossal statue known as El Cristo Rey, "Christ the King." It is in sight for many miles along the highway, and here shows prominently, though ten miles distant by airline. The recent erection of this statue is another indication of the increasing ecclesiastical influence in Mexico, from its point of furthest decline during the Revolutionary period of the twenties and thirties. This particular site was selected, not only because it is widely visible, but also because it is approximately the geographical center of the republic.

The rough and rather hazardous road leading to the statue is visible on the mountainside.

This picture was taken on the highway, about a mile south of Silao, and contains much that is worth notice in addition to El Cristo Rey. . . . Just what the ice-cream man with his pushcart was doing so far from town, I am not sure. In any case, his is a common Mexican trade, and he is a typical-enough Mexican figure, the darkness of his skin proclaiming almost pure Indian blood. This is not a point at which tourists are likely to stop, and he was much interested in my taking the picture. In fact, without being asked, he wanted to be a part of it, and posed himself, thus presenting some critical problems of focus, not easily solved with a four-by-five camera. Fortunately, the late afternoon sun was still bright, and the picture taken largely as a pious hope proved to be a useful one.

One should note that the ice-cream man, though a somewhat nondescript figure, represents modern rather than traditional Mexico. Except for the *huaraches* on his feet, he is wearing factory-made clothes, and his hat is scarcely a sombrero. Also, he has equipped his pushcart with pneumatic tires.

Beyond, one sees a common scene — the women doing the laundry at whatever outdoor water supply is available. Here they are washing at a large pool of water which has collected from the rains and been impounded behind the railway embankment to be seen on the farther side. Clothing is spread upon the bushes to dry. The children, who have accompanied their mothers, have all turned to look at the photographer, and one boy is approaching to investigate.

The skinned and eroded appearance of the ground across which the boy is walking is somewhat deceptive. As often in Mexico, earth has been stolen to build up the highway. This valley is well-watered, and productive, as the many trees indicate, and cornfields stretch off in the distance among the trees, and even well up the slopes of the mountain.

⓫ Celaya

• Mexico appeals largely to the tourist for its old-fashioned charm of plodding burros and white-garbed "peasants." These days, however, even such a thoroughly "colonial" city as Celaya has become an interesting mixture of old and new. The neat uniforms of the three little girls, returning from school at the noon hour, are as characteristic of modern Mexico as any other costume you might select. Also typical of modern Mexico in the scene are the paved streets, the elaborate lampposts, the tightly parked cars, and the signs advertising soft drinks, glassware, electrical fixtures, and sporting goods.

On the other hand, this view of the plaza, just after the noon whistle has blown, also shows a more ancient stratum. This is to be seen in the fine arcades, *portales,* at the left — a very practical feature, offering shelter both from sun and from showers. Many of the buildings in view have the appearance of dating back to the eighteenth century. Particularly fine is the one at the opposite side, with the flat-arched arcades and the balcony of iron grill-work.

At the right, the thickly set trees yielding heavy shade are more what is to be expected in the well-ordered Mexican plaza than are the closely cropped spheres of Encarnación de Díaz (see Picture 9). Equally in the tradition are the cast-iron seats, and the shoe-shine boy on his knees.

In the background stands the famous church of Nuestra Señora del Carmen — its richly adorned side-portal deftly placed to face the end of the street, its tiled dome and single tower rising against the skyline. Built in 1803-1807, it is the work of the most famous native Mexican architect, Francisco Eduardo Tresguerras. He was born in Celaya in the year 1745 of a prominent local family, never left his native country, and was seldom as much as a hundred miles away from his birthplace. Yet he practised so many arts with such success that he has been well termed the Michelangelo of Mexico.

The church here in view is generally considered his masterpiece. It might be called an example of late baroque at its best, with a strong classical influence. Mexico has been characterized as "a land of domes," and T. E. Sanford in his recent history of Mexican architecture selects this one as "the queen of them all."

After completing his masterpiece at the age of sixty-two, Tresguerras continued to live in Celaya until his death at the age of eighty-eight. Thus, curiously, one of the most fruitful and completely self-realized artistic lives of modern times was achieved in a small and isolated city by a man completely lacking in direct contacts with all the major influences of his times.

12 Bridge at the Río Laja

— Two miles east of Celaya, the highway crosses a stream of no great note in itself. Even when seen, as here, in the rainy season, the Laja is not a large river, though it must recently have been higher to have left such a neat sandbar breaking its surface. The bridge is more notable than the stream, being the work of the famous Tresguerras (see preceding picture).

That Michelangelo of Mexico was obviously an excellent engineer as well as an outstanding architect, thus to have bridged a stream which is subject, like most Mexican streams, to heavy floods. He bridged it not only beautifully but practically and permanently; his structure is still in use for the highway, as the passing truck indicates. The view is here upstream. The sharp-angled buttresses on this side are probably of little use, but on the other side they prevent the lodging of driftwood.

Bold, and yet economical — saving the construction of more piers — is the use of the flattened arches. Contrast, for instance, the massive, heavy-piered and high-arched bridge over the Esclavos River (see Picture 40).

Marking the end of the bridge are the only ornamental touches that the architect allowed himself. Looking a little like lions from a distance, these stone carvings are a pure composition of mingled curves suggestive of the elements used in baroque architecture. Their use in connection with a bridge is perhaps original.

Since its construction around the year 1800 the bridge seems to have drawn a word of comment from most of the travelers who have crossed it. Ward, in 1826, called it "magnificent"; Ruxton, in 1846, described it as "handsome," though he made the mistake of thinking that the river was the Lerma.

At the lower right, beneath the thick shade of an overarching tree, the inevitable woman is engaged at the never-ceasing labor of washing clothes. The traveler rarely passes a stream or even a muddy-looking rain-pool without seeing at least one of them at work.

In late morning the rainy-season clouds are just forming, but as yet give little suggestion of rain.

THE WAY TO GUATEMALA

Mexico City to the Border

Mexico 190, about 850 miles in length, lacks a traditional name, doubtless because few people in early times journeyed along its full length and conceived of it as a unified whole. It is here designated by a phrase drawn from the book written by one of its most famous earlier travelers, the Englishman, Thomas Gage.

Like the King's Road of the Interior, the Way to Guatemala can be

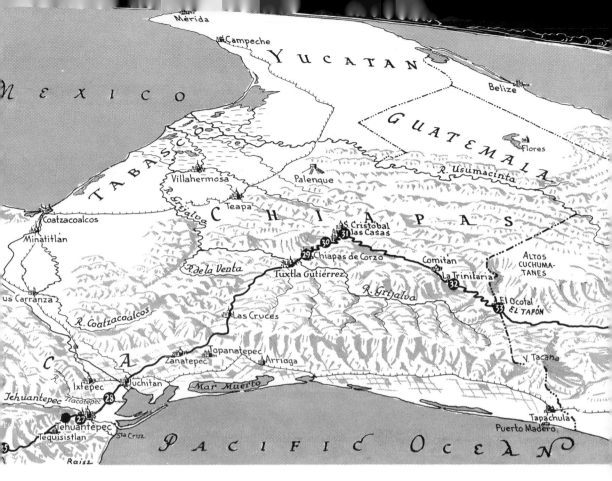

described as passing through an alternation of valley and mountain, but its contrasts are greater — the mountains, higher; the valleys, more sharply set off. Altitudes on the road range from almost sea level to more than ten thousand feet above. Correspondingly, the scenery is varied, ranging from the lowland tropics of the Isthmus of Tehuantepec and the district near the border to the Alpine regions between Mexico City and Puebla and near San Cristóbal.

The tourist is likely to enjoy this region the more, in addition, simply because it differs more from the United States. He may say that here is "the real Mexico," though a Mexican of the North would certainly resent such a characterization. Yet, it is true, the South has been less touched by modernity, less influenced by the United States and offers more "color." Perhaps the dividing line may be put at Puebla. Approximately at that point the solid, flat-topped adobe houses, typical of the North, begin to yield to the lightly built tropical huts with steeply pitched roofs of thatch. The other notable mark of the South is the use of oxen, instead of mules or horses, for plowing and hauling.

The Way to Guatemala offers some spectacular "sights." Departing from Mexico City toward the south, the tourist climbs rapidly into mountains, and can look down upon the famous valley. An hour later he descends into another valley near Puebla, and looks up at the perpetually snow-capped peaks of Ixtaccihuatl and Popocatepetl, two among the world's most beautiful mountains. Farther south, the road winds spectacularly through the rugged canyons of the Tehuantepec River, and offers sweeping views of the distant Pacific Ocean.

In the works of man the Way to Guatemala is also rich. It passes through two of the most renowned of Mexican cities, Puebla and Oaxaca. Actually visible from the highway are the great pyramid of the Cholula, the mountain-crowning ruins of Monte Alban and the tree of Tule. Scarcely less notable are such sights as the hilltop shrine of San Miguel at Atlixco, and the amazing Gothic churches of Huejotzingo and Yanhuitlán.

Finally, all along the road, the tourist from the United States observes people and ways of life that are new and interesting to him. He may, indeed, be disappointed in Tehuantepec. He can still see some of the colorful Tehuana costumes, and the women have not lost their stately grace of movement. The building of the highway, however, has ended their custom (praised by early travelers) of bathing naked in the river. But if Tehuantepec has become sophisticated, the Indian country that stretches from Chiapa de Corzo to Comitán has not yet had time to alter much, and the colorfully costumed men now walk on the highway, as they previously followed the trails.

After leaving Mexico City, the automobilist first goes eastward through the Valley of Mexico itself for some twenty miles. He then must climb, sharply and steeply, around many sweeping curves, to a summit which lies at 10,486 feet above sea level. The road then descends into the broad valley surrounding Puebla, and continues through connecting valleys to the south for a distance of about seventy-five miles — past the church-studded country around Cholula, through Atlixco and Matamoros.

Beyond this point the road winds up into a rugged region, infertile and thinly inhabited, except where it opens into some small valley. The mountains are not high, but they are sufficiently rough to make the road very winding and slow. The highway keeps to this broken country for a distance of no less than two hundred miles, until it drops into the famous valley of Oaxaca. This furnishes a pleasant break of forty miles, where the road is generally straight, bordered by cultivated fields, and busy with ox-carts, strings of burros, and people going to market.

Then the highway again enters the mountains, where it climbs and descends and twists and bends back upon itself, threading its way through defiles, and crossing many summits. This stretch extends for 120 miles, until the road descends almost to sea level and emerges on the Isthmus of Tehuantepec, only a few miles from the Pacific Ocean. Here the highway runs almost straight, and it is wide and well paved for about ninety miles.

The possibility of rapid progress ends sharply, at Tapanatepec, as the road again enters rugged mountains, climbing steeply and tortuously to a mile-high altitude. The view opens out, and the tourist sees to the south the great Pacific lagoon known as the Mar Muerto, "the dead sea." After thirty miles the road emerges into a rolling plateau region, across which it passes for the next ninety miles. At a point a few miles beyond Chiapa de Corzo, the highway can only be described as running head-on into the abrupt escarpment of mountains at the top of which lie the highlands of Chiapas. Once more the road twists and winds wildly, for forty miles, attaining an altitude of more than seven thousand feet.

Beyond San Cristóbal the 115 miles to the border may be divided into an 85-mile stretch of plateau country, then a ten-mile drop-off, and a twenty-mile *finale* across flat and tropical lowlands, to the border.

In its origins Mexico 190 is very ancient. It follows the line of a pre-conquest trail, used in the time of the Aztecs and even long before the arrival of those comparative newcomers to Mexico.

In that uncertain antiquity of Middle America which is peopled by such names as Mayas, Zapotecs, and Mixtecs, active trade was carried on by means of well-established routes. As scholars believe, one of the most important of these — what might even then have been called the Way to Guatemala — led southward from central Mexico. This route offered alternates at either end; a single road, in the middle. From the then populous city of Cholula one branch reached Oaxaca by a route very close to that of the present highway. The other branch swung more to the east, passing through Tehuacán, and following the route of the railroad. The two trails united near Etla, at the head of the Valley of Oaxaca.

A single trail continued through the valley, doubtless sending branches off to Monte Alban and Mitla in the days of their glory, and passing (any time within the last two thousand years) a cypress tree which still stands in the village called by the Spanish name of Tule. At the end of the valley the trail entered the hills, and worked its way through much rugged country, making use of the easiest passes. From the crest north of Totolapan anyone taking a moment to stop and look southward can see the remains of several older roads descending the mountainside. What is actually to be observed may not be very old, but there can be little doubt but that the ancient trail made use of the same natural pass and that later roads, in many places, follow the line of the old foot-trodden path.

The ancient traders' route went on, along the general line of the highway — to Tehuantepec and then across the flatlands of the isthmus. At Tapanatepec the trail again split into alternates. The right-hand branch, favored in the dry season, kept to the coastal plain, passing through the towns now served by the railroad. But when the rains came, the rivers rolled down in spate, and the jungles became quagmires. Then the Indian traders took to the highlands, and followed a route which was probably very close to that of Mexico 190, and which, like the coastal road, eventually led to Guatemala.

One should not, however, think of this ancient trail in terms of a modern highway. The men of those early civilizations were great builders; at Monte Alban they have left the ruins of a "civic center" that dwarfs the Roman Forum. But they built no roads to be compared with the Appian Way or Watling Street. There was no need. These early Americans made no use of wheeled vehicles, and even lacked beasts of burden. Their goods were transported, man-back, by long strings of bearers.

The *conquistadores* used the trails, and found them practicable for horses and even for the small cannon of that time. Spain itself is mountainous, and has been a country notable for bad roads; doubtless these Castilian and Biscayan soldiers found the trails about as good as the roads at home. Thus we should judge by means of the "argument from silence" —that Cortez in his dispatches to Charles V made no comment upon difficulties of roads during his advance inland, in spite of the mountains. His incidental references indicate that he was following wide and well-established trails, supplied with at least some bridges. He once mentions the "king's road," thus making a distinction between main and secondary thoroughfares.

The Aztec nobles were accustomed to traveling these trails on litters, borne by as many as eight men. Any trail that could accommodate such an equipage must have been almost practicable for an ox-cart. As for Cortez's cannon, these consisted of four light "falconets," and some heavier "lombards." In European armies of the time such pieces were drawn by ox-teams. Bernal Díaz in his reminiscences records that Cortez obtained bearers for them from the Indian allies — on one occasion one hundred; on another, two hundred. Díaz also mentions, though he makes no point of it, that the cannon were "carried." This suggests that some kind of apparatus like a litter was rigged up, so that a sufficient number of bearers could carry each gun. The Indians would have taken better to carrying than to pulling, since that was what they were used to. As far as evidence on the roads is concerned, it makes little difference. The number of men necessary to carry a lombard would have required at least as good a road as the same number of men hauling the same gun.

In their expeditions toward the south, from 1521 onward, the Spaniards also followed the established routes. Naturally they soon learned the tremendous difference between a Mexican trail in the dry season, and in the wet. Cortez mentions, for instance, that Rangel's expedition toward the south in 1523 returned after two months, without having accomplished anything "on account of its being the rainy season."

Very different is the record of Alvarado's expedition which left Mexico City on December 6, 1523, well after the ending of the rains. This was Alvarado's second foray in this direction, and possibly he had seen to it during the previous march that bad spots on the trail had been improved for the passage of his artillery. In addition, he himself was famous even among the *conquistadores* as a hard-driving commander. These explanations are offered to make credible what otherwise could scarcely be believed.

His army consisted of both foot and horse, and was encumbered by four cannon and "a large quantity of powder and other munitions of war," so that there must have been a long file of bearers. Notwithstanding, Alvarado arrived in the province of Tehuantepec, having covered a distance of approximately five hundred miles, on the thirty-eighth day. The over-all average daily march was thus about thirteen miles! This is a truly amazing feat, especially since much of it was across very rough mountains. Such a march is good evidence that the ancient trail was in excellent condition and offered few obstacles, even for artillery.

Cortez's fourth dispatch (1524) contains his only reference to road-building. Work, he stated, was being done between the seacoast and Mexico City, "that the transportation of goods may be facilitated by having a better road." Probably this means that the old trail was being made usable for wheeled vehicles.

Mendoza, the first viceroy of New Spain, was much interested in roads. During his term of office (1535-1549) the old trail to the south was improved clear to Tehuantepec. This may mean that it was made passable for wheeled vehicles, at least, for light artillery. But the evidence is not certain. Even if the road was thus improved by a burst of energy under a capable viceroy, this meant little for the future. In the mountains between Oaxaca and Tehuantepec yearly maintenance would have been necessary to keep the way open, because of earthquakes and tropical rainstorms.

The improvement by Cortez of the road between Mexico City and the coast becomes part of the history of the Way to Guatemala since included in it must have been the section between Mexico City and Puebla. At a somewhat later date three roads connected these two cities. The one farthest south was that which Cortez had followed in his original march; it passed between the peaks of the two great volcanoes, and attained altitude of more than 12,000 feet. The one farthest to the north made a circuit, going around the end of the mountain range; this was the cart-road. The middle road passed through Río Frío, thus following the line of Mexico 190, the Pan-American Highway. This road was the one most used by ordinary travelers, on foot and on horseback. Even in early times, moreover, part of this road was opened up for wheeled traffic, because much timber was cut in these mountains and had to be carted to Mexico City.

Father Berbolí Cobo, a Jesuit, who crossed that way early in 1630, was delighted with this forested country, which contrasted with the cactus-grown hills he had just traversed in coming from Oaxaca. "All this mountain," he wrote, "is a very thick forest of extremely tall and big pines, which make the view most pleasing." The virgin forest supplied much larger trees than any to be seen growing there now, and from some of the trunks Cobo saw the workmen fashioning big canoes, to be used on the lake which then filled a large part of the Valley of Mexico. He noted one dug-out so large that it had to be carried on a vehicle drawn by six yoke of oxen. The road must have been straight and well-designed to allow such a long team to be used on it.

Eventually this middle road, which Cobo said was called "of Río Frío," became the main highway from the port of Vera Cruz to Mexico City, and thus really the main highway of all the country. Innumerable travelers passed over it, always exclaiming at the view which opened before them as they first saw the Valley of Mexico. The road formerly must have given a better outlook than it does now, and in addition the valley was not covered by a pall of smoke and smog as it now is, being the habitation of close to three million people.

The devil-may-care Ruxton, near the beginning of his adventurous journey in 1846, went that way in a stagecoach. Like Cobo, he noted that it was a beautiful country, but he was chiefly interested in the pine-forest because it was notorious as the haunt of bandits. A mounted escort accompanied the coach, and we can imagine the adventure-loving Englishman inspecting his pistols, and rather unhappy that no bandits offered themselves as targets. "The road," he wrote, "is lined with crosses, which here are veritable monuments of murder perpetrated on travelers." (Crosses still stand by the Mexican highways, but now as memorials to travelers killed in motoring accidents.)

Much could be written about this section of the highway, but since it constitutes only a small fraction of the whole, we can only, like too many tourists, hurry onward.

In a sense, the real Way to Guatemala begins at Puebla, where the highway enters the Mexican southland. We are fortunate in having two early travelers' accounts, which together establish the line of the road and supply some description of almost all of it in the early seventeenth century.

As to the middle section and much of the northern, we can again draw upon the narrative of Father Cobo, who journeyed northward in the dry season of 1629-30. Having followed the coastal road from Guatemala, he noted its junction with the highland road near Tapanatepec, and then followed it on. He kept a careful log, noting the names of towns and the distances from one to the other. The towns, when identifiable, are those through which the highway now passes.

Thus traveling, Cobo came on through Oaxaca, and clear to Acatlán. At that point, however, he branched off to the east. Apparently this was the main road at that time; by taking this route it avoided the long stretch of mountainous and largely uninhabited country between Acatlán and Matamoros.

Aside from this valuable testimony as to the route, Cobo records rather little about traveling-conditions. His interest was in towns and convents. Making use again of the "argument from silence," we should conclude that his failure to mention anything about the road itself suggests that it made no great impression on his mind, presumably being just about what he expected, neither better nor worse. He traveled mule-back, and probably there was no through traffic of wheeled vehicles, although ox-carts may have been used in the vicinity of towns such as Tehuantepec and Oaxaca.

At one point on the isthmus he overtook a trail-herd of three thousand steers being driven to Mexico City. This shows at least that there was some traffic on the road, but Cobo records the incident only for a personal reason. The passing of the cattle, it seems, had scared up some rabbits, and three of these had become confused, dashed into the herd, and been trampled to death. Cobo bought one of them from the *vaqueros* for his supper.

The other traveler of this period was, like Cobo, a priest, but a much more famous person, chiefly because of his *New Survey of the West Indies*, part of which describes this very journey. This was Thomas Gage — a man, to my mind, more notable than admirable — deserter, venal priest, turncoat, and informer. Yet, as the fraternity of writers must unfortunately grant, a person can be all these things, and yet wield a ready pen.

An English Catholic, he came to Mexico in 1625 as one of a company of Dominican friars on their way to undertake missionary work in the Philippine Islands. Frightened at tales of hardships to be undergone, he and three others deserted in Mexico City, and set out under cover of night to flee southward by a circuitous route. In this first part of the journey, Gage is very hazy as to where he went, doubtless because he was traveling partly by night, and because he kept away from towns in fear of being apprehended and sent back. By the time he had arrived at Oaxaca, however, he had lost his fears, and from this point onward his report is clear.

Gage stayed three days in "Guaxaca," as the common spelling then was, liking it very much. There he and his companions got some news to rejoice their rascally hearts, that is, that by an order of the High Justice, the Indian towns along the road were required to give hospitality to traveling friars, and even to supply them with horses or mules. From this point on, therefore, Gage lived very comfortably, availing himself of the advantages of his cloth, even though he had shirked its responsibilities. Thus he traveled the well-beaten road, across the mountains to Tehuantepec, and over the isthmus until he arrived at Tapanatepec, the parting of the ways.

It was the dry season, and he could have traveled by the coast road, but he and his companions wished to go to San Cristóbal because they had heard that the Dominican prior there was a good fellow who would pardon their desertion and restore them to standing. The trouble about taking that road was that they would have to cross a rugged mountain, as the highway still does. This was also the season of the high winds which sweep down from the north across all that country of the Isthmus. Still, the attractions of the prior drew them on, and the worst of the distance across the mountain was only twenty miles.

They left Tapanatepec on a Sunday afternoon, and spent a pleasant night part way up the mountain. Next morning the wind was so high that they could not make progress against it, and holed up in a little shelter beside a spring. As Gage, dipping his pen deeply and collecting a classical allusion to adorn a fine seventeenth-century sentence, put the matter:

> Thither we went with much ado, hoping the wind would fall, but still the higher we climbed, the stronger we felt the breath of Aeolus, and durst not like the people called Psylli (of whom Herodotus writeth) march against him, lest as they found a grave in the sands where they met to oppose him, so we instead of ascending should by a

furious blast be made to descend into those deep and horrid preci-
pices, which truly threatened death, and offered to be a grave unto our
torn and mangled bodies.

In the shelter by the spring they spent the rest of that day and all the
night, only to find the wind growing stronger on Tuesday morning. They
were out of food, except for a little corn meal which their Indian guides
had brought along and for a few lemons which they found growing near-
by. Apparently becoming completely demoralized, they cowered beneath
the wind all day Tuesday and Wednesday, half starving, and finally beginning to despair of their lives.

On Thursday, they pulled themselves together in desperation, and
though the wind was still as high as ever, they mounted and went upward.
At some steep and narrow places, they walked and led their mules. Near
the top, they had to pass along a steep side-slope, the mountain rising
precipitously on the left and falling off on their right, with the ocean in
view. The exact situation, however, is difficult to make out, since Gage's
language is rhetorical rather than descriptive, giving the impression that
the travelers were in danger of being blown off the mountain and into the
ocean. In any case, they eventually won through. In all this account of
the mountain passage, we must conclude, Gage exaggerated greatly. The
ocean, instead of lying at the foot of the precipice, is a good ten miles away.

Continuing on, Gage made no mention of Tuxtla (only grown to be
important in recent times), but was delighted at the large Indian town
of Chiapa de los Indios (now, Chiapa de Corzo). On the other hand, he
considered Chiapa Real (San Cristóbal) to be "one of the meanest cities
in all America." Nevertheless he stayed there, making his peace with the
prior, and being re-established in his order. Toward the end of September
he traveled on, through Comitán, and eventually to Guatemala.

From Gage's account we gather the picture of the road in the seventeenth century as being a well-established mule-trail. He nowhere, however, notes wheeled traffic. He comments on the brisk trade in salt fish from
Tehuantepec northward to Oaxaca, Puebla, and Mexico City, and mentions meeting with these mule-trains "sometimes with fifty, sometimes
with a hundred mules together." Even close to the Guatemala border he
describes the road as "being much used and beaten by travelers." Here
also the goods were carried by long pack-trains, each consisting "of fifty
or three score mules."

In Gage's time the road was close to its height of activity. The Spanish colonies were still prosperous, and the activity of English and Dutch pirates encouraged travel by land. In the last half of the seventeenth century, however, depression set in, and thereafter the colonies stagnated.

An old saying runs, "Happy are the people whose annals are brief." If it is so with roads, this one must have been a very happy one, after the time of Gage and Cobo. The little evidence available rather indicates that it broke down into sections as trade declined, and really ceased to be a through road. We are thus forced to pass over a dark and uneventful period of more than two hundred years.

Apparently the Way to Guatemala was not wholly opened up for wheeled traffic. Humboldt, writing of the year 1803, placed the end of the road in the vicinity of Oaxaca, and considered that beyond that point only mule-trails passed through the mountains to Tehuantepec.

In 1865, under Maximilian, a catalogue and description of Mexican roads was published. At this time the main route from Puebla to Oaxaca was by Tehuacán, but an alternate followed the line of the present high-way. In the mountains beyond Oaxaca the road was described as impassable for vehicles.

Beyond Tehuantepec this same catalogue notes cart-roads in the flat country and only mule-trails in the mountains, as far as San Cristóbal. Beyond that town only distances are given, not descriptions, as if those who wrote the report had not traveled there.

The mid-nineteenth century brought some days of excitement. . . . In 1847 the Way to Guatemala was subjected to the tread of what Mexican orators call "Northamerican invaders." Not only did Scott march from Vera Cruz to Puebla and thence to Mexico City, but also the Americans penetrated along the road southward.

On the morning of October 18, to be exact, General Joseph Lane moved out from Puebla with 1500 men, including the Fourth Ohio, the Fourth Indiana, four companies of the First Pennsylvania, a squadron of the Third Dragoons, and some artillery. War had not yet lost all its glamor, and the regiments marched to the sound of fife and drum. The sun was hot, and snow-capped Popocatapetl loomed up ahead, as the column took the road for Atlixco.

After marching fifteen miles, about four o'clock, the boys were foot-sore and caked with sweaty dust, but a rattle of musketry brought them to life. The dragoons, out ahead, were fighting with Rea's guerrillas, the only Mexican troops in the vicinity — and these were as much bandits as troops and about as obnoxious to law-abiding Mexicans as to Northamerican invaders. When the infantry came up, the guerrillas retreated. Now the sharp conical hill at Atlixco stood up against the skyline ahead. After more skirmishing, Lane halted his troops at the edge of the town, a little after sunset. The guns were swung into position; after an hour of softening-up, the infantry advanced, just as a full moon was rising. They found only the civil authorities, eager to surrender. Rea and his guerrillas had galloped off, down the road to Matamoros, leaving their dead and wounded behind.

Next day the Americans marched back to Puebla, not without taking with them (it is, unfortunately, stated by some authorities) many souvenirs in the form of liberated Atlixcan valuables.

The indefatigable Lane set out again southwards on the evening of November 22, with two hundred mounted men. Next day he was in Matamoros, and two days after that was back in Puebla, having marched a hundred miles, been victorious in several skirmishes, destroyed a stock of munitions, and liberated some prisoners of war.

Rea's guerrillas, who had been making a nuisance of themselves, suffered some casualties and a considerable shattering of morale in these two encounters, and after this time are not prominent in history's pages. Mexican sentiment, however — naturally enough — has transformed these bandit-like guerrillas into self-sacrificing defenders of the Fatherland, and a simple shaft, now standing beside the road, commemorates them.

As for the highway itself, all that Lane's expeditions let us know is that a road, passable for artillery, extended as far as Matamoros, and that there was a bridge north of Atlixco. One of the skirmishes was fought at a bridge, which may, indeed, be the broken one still to be seen at one of the ravines.

The building of a railroad, as always, decreased the importance of the road. In this area the effect was a peculiar one. One line was built to Oaxaca from the north, and another line came down from Vera Cruz to Tehuantepec. No railroad was ever built, however, between Tehuantepec and Oaxaca, so that those two cities were more isolated, one from the other, in the early twentieth century than they had been in the seventeenth.

In 1902 Hans Gadow, the naturalist, set out from Tehuantepec northward in the rainy season. The road was not considered passable during the rains, but this particular year had been unusually dry, and Gadow went through to Oaxaca without difficulty. He was on horseback, but started with an ox-cart for his baggage. At some point, he must have sent the cart back, for he mentions hiring pack-mules. There were no bridges, and traffic was limited to occasional trains of mules and burros, on local business. Gadow's comments show that the country along the road, as well as the road itself, was extremely primitive.

During the same period all the Chiapas highlands remained in primeval isolation. No railroad was ever built into that region, and until recently anyone in San Cristóbal wishing to get to the outside world had to ride a horse for five days to reach Arriaga, the nearest point on the railroad.

After 1930 Mexico embarked upon its modern road-building program, which has so greatly transformed the Mexican way of life. The advance of the roadheads into the South, however, was very slow.

In 1931 the Automobile Club of Southern California sent a pioneering expedition southward. It consisted of six men under the leadership of E. E. East, traveling in three light trucks with spare parts and such accessories as rope and block-and-tackle. They left Mexico City on February 6, and five days later got to Oaxaca. They went on, confidently, believing that they could follow an old cart-road to Tehuantepec. After 52 miles, which should have taken them a little beyond Totolapan, at a place called San Juanico, they came to a full stop.

Nevertheless they did not give up. They obtained the cooperation of the governor of the state, and he assigned forty laborers to help build road and get the trucks through. Recording distances to tenths of miles, the trail-breakers moved on. One day they made 3.5 miles; then, 5.1; then, 2.5. In advancing the 17.5 miles they crossed the river 88 times, often having to pull the trucks through with block-and-tackle. In getting over the Cuesta de Burros (Jackass Hill, it would be in California) they made .3 miles in one day, and .7 the next; in five days, 5.5 miles.

At one point they almost despaired. By exploring, however, they found an old *camino real,* and were able to continue. After *fifty days* they arrived in Tehuantepec.

Without much difficulty they went across the isthmus as far as the historic parting of the ways at Tapanatepec. There they left the present line of the highway, taking the old dry-weather route through Arriaga. Eventually they went on into Central America.

Their historian claims that this was "perhaps, the most strenuous journey ever undertaken by ordinary automobiles." The present writer has no great desire to dispute this claim. It might, however, be pointed out that this expedition was well financed and magnificently equipped, and had official cooperation from the State of Oaxaca. Its achievement is thus possibly less notable than those of some of the private expeditions (see pp. 23-26).

These explorers were convinced, not only that no cart-road existed in 1931, but also that none had ever existed. One does not like to argue with experts who were actually there to see. Still, their own discovery, farther on, of a *camino real* raises some doubts. One can point out, again, that those mountains are subject to violent earthquakes and to torrential downpours, so that the complete disappearance of sections of a once established road would not be beyond possibility.

I myself, in a very small way, may set up a claim to being a pioneer automobilist along the Way to Guatemala. . . . Early in 1938, in full dry season, I set out with my wife one day to drive the hundred miles from Puebla to Cuernavaca by way of Atlixco, Matamoros, and Cuautla. The road was paved as far as Atlixco. Thence to Matamoros, we followed approximately the line of the present highway, but on an entirely different surface.

It was one of those roads which can still be seen here and there (see Picture 22) running parallel to the paved highway and still being used by herdsmen for their sheep and cattle. Such roads were generally broad and well-enough laid out, and had bridges, but they had little or no surfacing, so that they were impassable in the wet season for a car.

We bumped slowly along on the old-time road the twenty-some miles from Atlixco to Matamoros. Being in a 1937 model we took the chuck-holes and straddled the high crowns easily enough, not scraping bottom as we would in a present-day car.

At Matamoros we turned off to the west, and so left the line of Mexico 190. The road was, however, about the same that we would have had, I imagine, if we had tried to go on southward. It was, in short, scarcely a road at all. At one point it turned and calmly proceeded down a railroad track for a hundred yards. Little side-roads kept running off, and they were not appreciably worse than the "main road."

In such a situation there is always the possibility of taking the wrong track, and so I kept asking the direction of every countryman I saw along the way. Usually I asked if I was headed for Jonacatepec, and how long it would take me to get there. I knew it was only about twenty miles from Matamoros to Jonacatepec, and so I was set back when I had already driven at least ten miles and yet kept getting a reply "About two hours!" I soon figured out that these people had not the slightest idea about automobiles, and were only answering how long it would take them to walk the distance.

Eventually, after a final two miles of incredibly rough road, we got to Jonacatepec, went ahead, came at length to the river at Cuautla, forded it, and then had a dusty gravel road to our destination.

An official Mexican road map of approximately the same time that I drove to Matamoros shows that south of that point there was no continuous road which could be considered passable for automobiles, or even, I should say, for trucks. Since the jeep had not yet been invented, we might say that there was no passable road at all. There were short stretches of graveled road on both sides of Oaxaca, and a similar road from the railroad at Arriaga across to Tuxtla.

But the Mexican highway program was developing rapidly. The republic had come to realize the importance of automobile roads, not only to bring the tourist dollar in, but also to activate the economic life of the various regions. War brought further stimulation, and in 1942 Mexico passed a record budget for construction. The highway was pushed south, hopefully to connect with the road which the U. S. Engineers were starting to build in Central America as an overland link to the Panama Canal. Almost exactly along the line of the centuries-old Indian trail, the highway advanced. In 1943 Oaxaca was linked up. Then came Tehuantepec; then, Tuxtla. Though the United States lost interest in the highway for defence purposes, Mexico continued work. By 1946 a passable road ran clear to Comitán, and thus even Chiapas had lost its immemorial isolation.

On May 22, 1950, President Alemán, in a ceremony at Tehuantepec, officially opened the road clear to the Guatemala border.

13 Cuts and Shrines

— Twenty-eight miles from Mexico City along the road toward Puebla, at a spot high in the mountains known as El Corazón "the heart," the highway passes through some remarkably deep cuts. The bank at the right rises almost perpendicularly to a height of about 60 feet.

Such cuts are, indeed, a striking feature of the road south of Mexico City, clear into Central America. They seem to be adapted to the deposits of volcanic material, which is able to maintain itself in such a cliff, although not consolidated into rock. Many of these cuts were excavated by hand labor, and possibly the ones in view were at least so finished off. The projecting boulders speak for a delicacy of work scarcely possible with machines.

Occasionally to be seen along Mexican highways are shrines to the Virgin, such as these at the right of the road. A workman is engaged at some repairs of one of them, standing upon the usual ramshackle scaffolding to which Mexicans habitually entrust their lives. Not only are these shrines being kept in good repair, but they are also well-built, with much tile, and elaborately adorned with fresh flowers. The smaller niche at the right shows the position of an original, simple one, which has yielded to the present more elaborate constructions.

Although these shrines are probably maintained and invoked chiefly by truckers as a means of protection for themselves on the highway, a traffic engineer would undoubtedly be concerned with the hazard thus created by their intrusion at this narrow point.

The steep mountainside seen in the background has been largely denuded of trees by lumbering and fire, but some live pines along with several prominent dead ones show on the skyline. Under better conditions these mountains would be magnificently forested, and some protection to the trees in this area along the highway would soon be rewarded by the appearance of a more healthy forest and by the greater attraction offered to tourists.

⑭ Popo and Ixta

✚ Popocatepetl and Ixtaccihuatl, once thought the highest peaks of Mexico, are now known to be exceeded in altitude by Citlaltépetl (18,855 feet), but remain the most famous of Mexican mountains because of their proximity to the capital and the main highway. Their beauty is much enhanced by their paired quality, which sets them in continually varying relationships, as the motorist changes his angle of view. The two are so intimately a part of Mexican life that natives and tourists alike refer to them as Popo and Ixta.

The mountains are here seen from the east, from a point on the road about five miles out of Puebla on the way south. Ixta, the more northern of the two, thus appears on the right — not on the left, as it does when seen from Mexico City. Its peak is about 25 miles away; that of Popo, about five miles nearer.

The Fujiyama-like cone of Popo rises to a height of 17,888 feet above sea-level, that is, to about 11,000 feet above the point from which the picture was taken. Since this was just the end of the season of warm rains, the remarkably even snow-line lies high, probably at 16,000 feet; the timber-line can be made out, about 2000 feet lower. Popo is still true to its name "smoke-mountain." It remains active as a volcano, and a suggestion of smoke or steam hangs about its crest in the picture. Lower down the slope a small cloud has formed, trailing off to the southward.

Ixta (17,343 feet) displays a more extensive snow field along its ridge. Its name means "white woman," and it must therefore have been named by people who saw it from another direction. From the angle of the picture only the whiteness is observable, unless one wishes to imagine an extremely deformed female. The small pointed peak at the right is the one which from Mexico City gives the suggestion of a woman's upturned face.

The pass between the two peaks, though it is over 12,000 feet high, was used by an Aztec road and Cortez made his first entry to the valley of Mexico by this route.

In the foreground stretches the rich plain of which Puebla, the fourth city of Mexico, is the chief center of population. In Aztec times, the great and many-templed city of Cholula dominated the area. That present town, with its great pyramid, lies somewhat to the north, and out of the scope of the picture. This is, however, the Cholula district as is made evident by the elaborate church on the hill and the two other churches faintly visible in the distance. Cortez, in one of his dispatches, assured his master the emperor that from the top of one temple in Cholula it was possible to look around and count four hundred others. Since the conquerors, by policy, set out to replace temples with churches, this particular area is the most over-churched in Mexico, which is probably as much as to say, in the world.

Like the other flat lands of Mexico, the plain is planted almost solidly in corn, here standing dry in late October.

The highway here is an old one for Mexico, having been paved for twenty years or more. It displays, therefore, as is to be expected, an almost continuous succession of patches. Cheap labor makes it possible to mend individual breaks almost indefinitely, so that eventually one has trouble in finding any of the original surface.

The picture was taken about 8.30 A.M. The sun was not yet high enough to bring out contrasts, and a monotone suggestive of dawn lies over the landscape. Within half an hour the increasing heat of the sun had caused the small cloud already showing to build up into a mass which completely obscured the upper half of the peak. (Compare Picture 44.)

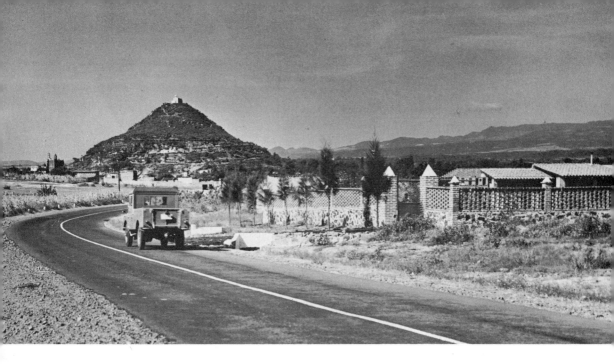

 Atlixco

✦ Worship in "high places," against which the Hebrew prophets protested, is a practice among many peoples, and the ancient Mexicans set their temples either upon artificial pyramids or upon pyramid-like hills, as here. At least such a temple is to be assumed from the present existence of a church. Typically, also, this is a church of San Miguel, or St. Michael — for, as Henry Adams puts it, "the Archangel loved heights."

The town itself lies at the foot of the hill to the left, where stands the church of St. Francis, a more intimate human saint, who preferred to live more closely with his fellow-creatures, not to withdraw from them in archangelical hauteur.

At the right, against a background which is the lower slope of Popocatepetl, may be seen a good example of modern Mexican *suburbia*, adorned with more stone-, brick-, and tile-work than any American suburbanite could afford. The wall around the property seems to represent a compromise. A wall, for protection and privacy, is in the Spanish and Mexican traditions. But a wall through which anyone can see, suggests the influence of the United States, where people build their houses exposed to full view. Perhaps, however, the open brickwork may be an economy measure, since building-costs in Mexico are not so cheap as they once were.

The lower picture displays the plaza of Atlixco. As in most Mexican towns, there is the mingling of traditional and modern. A simulated traffic-cop with raised hand, stands by an unpaved street, close to arcaded *portales* and under fine balconies projecting from buildings that go back at least to the Díaz era. Of the new age also are the traffic-pointers for one-way streets, and these contrast with the now rather rare Mexican of the old school, who wears a sombrero and a white suit, and has a *serape* thrown over one shoulder. He must be chiefly Indian in blood; his face is so dark that it blots out entirely under the shade of the broad brim.

The woman, against the background of advertisements for motion-pictures and beneath a telephone-cable, may be considered a transition figure. She carries her basket on her arm, not on her head, and her dress is apparently a factory product. But she sticks by her dark-colored *rebozo*.

The shrine of the Archangel — relic of the past or symbol of the present? — looks down upon it all.

16 Market and Church

● By now, in Izucar de Matamoras it is well on in the afternoon, and a line of heavy shadow lies halfway across the dirt street that serves for the highly typical outdoor market. So late in the day the market has been almost deserted; some children remain, and a few women, who linger on, still hoping to make a sale of sugar-cane or oranges, or of the soft drink which stands on the old wooden table in a glass jar, with a piece of ice melting beside it.

Across the way, flaps have been put down to shield the booths from the still torrid sun. But even fewer people linger on that side. Peppers, hung in bunches, form a design against the background of white cloth in the booth farthest to the left.

Even here, though it is farther south than Atlixco, everyone is wearing cheap factory-made clothes, except for the *huaraches* of the woman at the right. She is also wearing a *rebozo*.

Careful anatomical study reveals the fact that the arm which at first seems to be this woman's must belong to a child standing just behind her. Or else, if anyone thinks this is jumping to conclusions, she has three arms, one of them jointed at her hip.

In the background, the churchyard is enclosed by the inevitable tall columns connected with iron-work. The church itself, with its heavy, time-worn buttresses, is old, and may go back well toward the Conquest. The single tower looks newer, but even it is probably no more recent than the eighteenth century. Since southern Mexico is subject to earthquakes, high towers are rare, and this is one of the last ones that the southward-driving tourist can expect to see.

Although in the foreground the sun casts a sharp shadow, the sky in the background shows the chalky and monotonous overcast of an October day that is just on the edge, so to speak, of the wet and dry seasons. No massive and brilliantly white thunderheads are building up, to let loose with a downpour at four o'clock. (Compare Picture 23.)

 Ridge Road

✦ Many primitive trails follow ridges, and some modern highways do the same. The advantage lies in avoiding stream-crossings and in finding a comparatively level passage across what may be the remnant of some ancient peneplain. As evidenced by the picture, the disadvantage is the sinuous course often necessitated.

The scene is here a mountain crest, about 7500 feet above sea level, half-way between Nochixtlán and Huitzo in the state of Oaxaca.

The highway, although paved, requires cautious and slow driving, and in this respect is not much different from most of the road between Matamoros and Oaxaca. As traffic increases, the road will have to be straightened for safety. This will only repeat what has happened in the United States; for instance, in the twenties the Ridge Road (U.S. 99) out of Los Angeles toward the north looked very much like this. As in Picture 14, the patches in the pavement show clearly, though this pavement is probably less than ten years old.

The country shows the mixture of pine and oak which is widespread in this region at such an altitude. Logging, charcoal-burning, fires, and over-grazing have reduced the trees to scarcely more than a few scattered survivors. Along the highway in the distance erosion is evident. The Mexican government is already taking measures against charcoal-burning, but unless something is done quickly, such a region as this seems destined soon to become a maze of treeless and grassless gullies.

In the bare spot midway along the highway, some black spots indicate three burros whose sharp hoofs and gnawing teeth are helping with the erosion.

In the foreground, the remains of an old road sidle off along the hillside among the oaks. At the edge of the pavement run well-established paths where the grass has been worn away by people and animals following the road. Rarely in the United States is there enough of such travel to wear paths. Other such trails appear on the hillsides.

In the distance the skyline ridge probably tops 8000 feet, and a few low clouds rest upon it.

18 Oaxaca—Plaza

● The plaza is such an integral part of a Mexican town — and of Mexico — that an apology is scarcely needed for putting that of Oaxaca on record for comparison with those of Chihuahua, Encarnación de Díaz, Celaya, and Atlixco. (See Pictures 2, 9, 11, 15.)

As with most Mexican cities, automobile traffic has made one-way streets out of those that surround the plaza here. That is why everything is pointed in this direction, the street being actually Mexico 190 for northbound traffic. The automobile has forced burros and even horse-drawn wagons out of the picture, but not the bicycle. Six of these are visible. In contrast to trucks and bicycles is the little countryman in his traditional white suit.

The picture was taken almost at noon, but the magnificent trees cast a scarcely broken and very welcome shade. These are Indian fig-trees, not native to Mexico, but widely grown, and seeming to flourish as vigorously as the eucalyptus and other foreign trees flourish in California.

As generic traits of Mexican plazas may be noted the elaborate seats, the ornamental lampposts, the arcades, and the advertising signs. The arcade at the left shelters the street-cafe of the principal hotel, which thus becomes also the contact-point where natives and tourists dicker for *serapes* and other local wares.

⓲ Oaxaca—Street Scene

✚ Looking up any Mexican street, one is likely to see the view ending in mountains against the sky; if it is the rainy season, the summits will probably be cloud-capped, as here.

This particular street is Avenida Juárez, in Oaxaca, still the line of Mexico 190. The view is toward the north, but the highway has twisted about to enter the city, and an approaching car would actually be going south in order to go toward Mexico City, which lies to the north. Such anomalies, however, are by no means absent in our own cities also. Moreover, there is a by-pass (rare in Mexico, but becoming commoner) which removes the necessity of such meandering.

The plaza (see preceding picture) is about a quarter-mile off to the left. The business district lies in that direction also, and this is a residence street.

It looks like many others in the city, and in sister cities. Notable, because of the solid front of houses, is the sharp line between sun and shade — "sol y sombre." This is a very practical feature; except for a short period daily, you can walk in the shade, although in the picture about as many people are on the one side as on the other. Such a front forms an almost complete contrast to what may be expected in the residence district of a town in the United States, with its front lawns and widely spaced dwellings. Even though shade-trees may afford protection along one of our streets, much of the advantage still lies with Mexico. The concentration of population, for instance, makes transportation less of a problem. Moreover, these houses — as anyone can see by looking in at the doorways — open into secluded and often well-gardened patios. There is still much of the fortress about Mexican houses, with their single solidly doored portals opening on the street, and the heavy iron bars before the windows. Yet there can be cheer and hospitality inside; only the exterior is forbidding.

Houses in Mexico are generally low, and especially so in Oaxaca, which has been plagued with earthquakes, the last severe one in 1931. Probably all the buildings in this picture, except for their foundations, date from after that year. The ancient tradition of Mexican architecture thus was dominant in such outlying towns as this after modernism had begun to take over in Mexico City. Except for the ugly tower-like structure in the background, the buildings harmonize and produce a unified effect, as if springing from the craft of a city-planner.

"No anunciar" means "Post no bills," but the soft-drink sign seems to make light of this warning. Soft drinks, however, occupy a place of privilege in Mexico, and are often associated with official signs. The *Preferencia* arrow indicates that traffic from that direction has the right of way.

The radio aerials supply a semi-modern touch. Note, however, the buffer at the corner of the building, probably a survival from the time when there was no sidewalk, and the structure had to be protected against wheels.

The street-sweeper, with his primitive broom and neat pile of rubbish, serves to put life into the street scene, and provides a reminder that handwork still flourishes in Mexico. The backward-turning woman gives an indication of how unconscious of tourists Mexican cities like Oaxaca have become. She looked around to see what could interest the photographer.

This picture may be compared with 31, which permits some view inside similar houses.

20 Feeder Trail

✛ In Mexico, a step off the highway often equals a step backwards through a hundred years. Yet the cities live largely on the products that come in by ox-cart or by burro over these ancient trails.

The outlook is here from a point above the village of San Felipe, near Oaxaca. The line of the highway, not actually visible, enters from the right in the middle distance, and then curves to follow the valley, and finally passes through the hills about at the farthest rainstorm.

This particular trail is broad enough to be used by ox-carts, but it is very rough, and probably little work has ever been done on it. The passing of the animals has worn much of the protecting vegetation away; erosion has taken the thin soil of the hillside, and the bare rocks are showing in many places. If there is any depth of soil, such a trail will keep washing away until it is below the general level, as this one is doing toward the right of the picture.

The woodcutters, on their way down to town, are Zapotec Indians, though Christianized and Spanish-speaking. They have been to cut fire-wood in the mountains, which show as the background of the preceding picture, where their tribe owns an allotment of land. As compared with many Indians, they are therefore wealthy, and they have burros to carry the wood for them. (See Picture 36.) In costume they offer nothing distinctive, apparently making use of any odds and ends that are cheaply available, including on the left the ruins of a felt hat.

Much of the firewood is very small stuff, such as would not be marketable in the United States. But in Mexico, little is wasted.

The flower-stocks, arising to the size of small trees and not yet blooming, are from a plant of the agave family, of which the one most commonly known farther north is the maguey, or century-plant. This local variety is used in the manufacture of mescal, the southern-Mexican equivalent of tequila.

Beyond, cornfields cover the rolling lower slopes of the mountains, and merge into the cornfields of the valley. A small clump of darker color, just at the left of the agave stock on the left, is apparently the great tree of Tule (see the next picture). A distant view of the rich valley of Oaxaca is also afforded, which may be seen at closer range in Picture 22.

Although the intense and well-defined rainstorms on the distant mountains are what may be expected in the rainy season, the generally overcast sky and widespread clouds are not so common. At this time a hurricane was sweeping in against the Gulf coast, and even as far south as Oaxaca general rains were occurring.

21 Tree of Tule

● Six miles beyond Oaxaca is the village of Tule, insignificant in itself but renowned for one of the world's most magnificent trees.

A board standing near the base of the tree conveniently lets us know that it is an example of *Taxodium mucronatum*. The species is generally called Mexican cypress in English, and *ahuehuete* by the Mexicans themselves. This tree is approximately 2000 years old, 125 feet high, and 55 feet in diameter. Its trunk is estimated to weigh 300 tons. It may also be described as very beautiful, and still apparently growing with vigor. It is generally considered the largest tree in Mexico.

This tree had attained about three-quarters of its present age at the time of the Conquest, and must have seemed about as large to the first Spaniards as it does to us now.

As compared with the General Sherman tree, the giant of Sequoia National Park in California, the tree of Tule is almost twice as large at the base, but less than half as tall, and only about one third as heavy. The sequoia is estimated to be at least a thousand years older.

The setting of the tree is the village churchyard. Or, to put it more accurately, the church must have been located so as to include the tree in the churchyard, since the tree is so much older than the church. Again, as at Atlixco (see Picture 15), tall stone piers are connected with ironwork. The church itself is not without good architectural qualities; it displays the squat, solidly built towers necessary in earthquake-country. The small cupolas on the towers, show the tile-work particularly characteristic of churches in the Puebla area.

Though this village is so close to Oaxaca and is on the main highway, the woman crossing the highway is wearing a native costume. The picture was taken on a Sunday, when she had probably put on her finery.

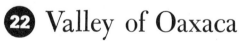

22 Valley of Oaxaca

✚ About fifteen miles beyond Tule, a great flat-topped rock rises a hundred feet sheer at the left of the road. From its top, in a southwest direction, the picture was taken.

Mexico is pre-eminently a land of mountain and valley; of the latter this is one of the most famous. Even in the time of the Conquest the beauty and richness of the country around Oaxaca was such that Cortez managed to have it assigned to him as a fief, and from it took his title as Marquis of the Valley. Though here only a small end or corner of the famous valley appears, its richness and the intensity of cultivation are obvious. Corn is the predominating crop. The fields are small, and informal hedge rows separate them, producing a pleasing and irregular checkerboard pattern.

The highway is here built up well above the general level to avoid flooding during the rainy season. Several miles of it are in view, as it heads toward the Mitla turn-off, which is slightly beyond the farthest point visible. There the highway swings farther toward the right, and passes through a low spot of the hills toward Tehuantepec. The inevitable bus, with baggage piled high on top, is headed in that direction. Several people appear on the highway, for in this thickly inhabited country such a stretch of road is seldom vacant.

What looks like a stream in the foreground and to the left of the highway is an old road. It was well laid off at one time, and was approximately as broad as the present highway. Use — in these later days, by droves of cattle and burro-trains — has worn it down and allowed erosion until water from the rains stands in it.

The valley here is about 5500 feet in altitude; the farther mountains, perhaps 3000 feet higher. The pass to the right, however, through which the highway passes, is only some 500 feet higher than the valley.

As in Picture 20, the general distribution of heavy clouds, in late morning, indicates that the hurricane is still active on the Gulf coast.

Organ Cactus

✛ Though the flat-leafed nopal cactus is honored on the Mexican flag, the tall organ cactus or saguaro is a nobler and more conspicuous plant, and is widely spread throughout the republic. It is also a notable feature of the landscape in southern Arizona. Growing, as here, on steep hillsides, it produces a strange perpendicular or lined effect to the landscape.

As the glaring highlights of the picture suggest, this is a dazzling noon of the rainy season, torridly hot and a little humid, with the thunderheads rising clean-cut against the dark sky. Baking in the full sun, the highway can be seen ascending the ravine ahead, shown by the raw scars of its cuts and the still ungrown-over debris of its fills.

This picture was taken at almost the same time of day as the preceding one, only a week later and at a spot not over 25 air-miles distant, but the atmospheric conditions are vastly different. In the meantime the hurricane had blown itself out, and ordinary rainy-season conditions had been re-established.

The location is a few miles to the south of Totolapan, and the altitude here is only about 3000 feet, the lowest point that the tourist from the north will as yet have experienced in Mexico. The low altitude, together with scanty rainfall, is reflected in the vegetation, with thorn-scrub filling the gaps between the cacti. This may also be called the most severe and inhospitable country yet to be encountered — torrid, parched, rough, and scarcely inhabited. There is little suggestion of grass, and no real trees can be seen.

Actually, at this time of year the country is a little better looking than it is in the dry season. Then many of the shrubs loose their leaves and there seems to be a general shrinking-in of vegetation, with the cacti standing out more prominently, as if the desert had moved in.

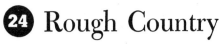 Rough Country

— As mentioned in the description of the preceding picture, the country between Oaxaca and Tehuantepec is extremely rough. The present picture gives further demonstration.

Here, about 12 miles south of the preceding picture-point and high above one of the branches of the Tehuantepec River, the road has been blasted out of the rock, at one point supported by a natural buttress, and at another by a high-built wall of masonry. Since this is fairly new construction the disturbed rock-face on the upper side has not yet had time to adjust itself, and two landslides have come down during the recent rainy season. Both of these endangered traffic at the time of their fall, and even now are scarcely cleared off. Road-maintenance in Mexico is not yet at the standard approved in the United States.·

In the distance the highway can be seen curving to the left, still following the line of the river, and then reappearing high up on the mountainside, where it has been forced to leave the canyon and to loop back on itself.

The extreme roughness of the country shown in this picture and in those which precede and follow it, fully explains the great difficulties encountered by the Automobile Club of Southern California expedition of 1931 and by the Richardson expedition of 1940-41. (See pages 25, 97.) Both these parties, however, managed to get through, by the process of building road as they proceeded and by liberal use of block-and-tackle. One questions whether such expeditions can really be called automobile trips. In many places the cars had to be handled as so much dead weight, and did not go ahead under their own power.

The altitude here is about 2500 feet, and the growth is thorn-scrub. Although this spot is close to that of the preceding picture, something in soil, exposure, or climate prevents the growth of cactus, and none is visible.

The picture was taken at the end of October, after the letting-up of the rains, and the river has receded, showing its sand-bars. Its recent high-water-mark is obvious from the expanse of rock which has been swept clear of soil and vegetation.

At this time of year one would expect a glaring hot day in this locality, but clouds have been swept down from the Gulf of Mexico by a north wind, and have mercifully veiled the sun.

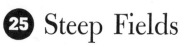 Steep Fields

— Nothing in Mexico is likely to impress the tourist more than the intense and yet necessarily inefficient attempts to wring a living from isolated and steep fields.

Here, a dozen miles south of El Camarón, still in the mountains between Oaxaca and Tehuantepec, we look from the highway upon one of these desperate ventures — a few acres of cultivation, in a vast expanse of rugged, scrub-covered mountains.

In the nearer field, corn is growing; in the farther one, maguey. Various varieties of the latter — known as the ornamental century-plant in the United States — are cultivated over much of Mexico on the drier lands for production of fibre and as a source of the national drinks — pulque, tequila, and mescal. (See also Picture 20.) As here, it produces a distinctive pattern in the landscape. In the farther fields, to the left, both corn and maguey are growing.

Most of these fields are too steep to hold their soil for long under cultivation. The maguey, which does not require disturbance of the top-soil is the better plant for such hillsides; cornfields erode rapidly. In the foreground of the picture, in fact, appears what is apparently a field which has been cultivated at no long time back, but has suffered erosion until now its surface displays many large boulders. It will have to be allowed to return to brush for an indefinite number of years or centuries. From the point of view of long-time national economy such farming may be termed suicidal, since it rapidly destroys the land.

The highway, after showing as a light-colored cut just above the field of maguey, continues on among the mountains, and in the distance may be seen curving around to the left as it ascends to the pass just at the left of the castle-like summit. Faint traces of a smaller road show at the left.

At the summit of the conical hill in the middle of the picture appears a small protuberance which does not look — in the photograph, at least — exactly like a tree or a rock. Such appearances, particularly on the top of conical hills, continually arouse one's curiousity in Mexico. In similar locations the ancient peoples constructed their temples. The chance of any ancient site being located in these barren mountains is, however, very unlikely.

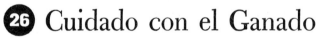 Cuidado con el Ganado

— Like "cattle" in English, "ganado" in Spanish generally means "cow-critters," but theoretically includes all livestock. The sign CUIDADO CON EL GANADO is certainly to be taken in the broader sense, since the driver rounding a corner in Mexico is likely to encounter almost any kind of domestic animal on the highway. The warning would seem literally to indicate "Be careful with the cattle," but "of" should doubtless be substituted in translation.

Here the animals happen to be goats, a whole flock of them, with many kids. They were largely up on the steep bank at the right, as a few of them still are, when the car disturbed them. Usually there is a herdsman with goats, but none is in evidence here. Like untended animals generally in Mexico, they consider the highway their own property. At least, there is little likelihood of hitting a goat; they are fast movers in an emergency.

This is more of the thorn-scrub country, close to the Tehuantepec River, and only about six miles south of the preceding picture. Goats do well enough in such country, because they are not grazers and so have no need of grass, but rear up on their hind legs to browse the leaves and twigs of bushes. Even the roughest country is no handicap to a goat.

Note, again, the fallen rocks on the highway at the foot of the cliff.

27 Waiting for the Bus—Hot Country

— Mexico has constructed a fine network of modern roads, but the standard of living is as yet too low to permit any widespread ownership of automobiles. The bus has therefore become a national institution.

Here an east- or southbound early-morning bus approaches a group of prospective passengers on the outskirts of the town of Tehuantepec. With the informality accompanying most Mexican travel, one passenger already stands on the running board of the bus, ready to jump off even before it stops.

The six people at the roadside display a variety in their costumes such as would hardly ever be equalled in the United States. The farther man is a soldier in uniform. The nearer man wears the traditional white pants and broad-brimmed hat, and carries a blanket-roll slung over his shoulder. Of the four women, the two on the left are wearing the local Tehuana costume, one of the most notable in Mexico. A third woman, however, has merely a factory-made dress with a handkerchief over her hair, and would pass without comment in any of our smaller towns. An old woman wears dark clothes suggestive of mourning, and with a native touch to their cut. Except for the one in store clothes, all the women wear skirts trailing almost to the ground.

The big baskets and the blanket-roll will be piled upon the already high-piled baggage on top of the bus, or stowed away somewhere else. The capacity of a Mexican bus seems to be unlimited. They serve in fact, as carriers of express and even of light freight. (For another example, see Picture 62.)

The landscape in the foreground, on both sides, is the well-watered bottomland of the Tehuantepec River, and displays a lushness not often seen along the highway, though in the background rises one of the usual scrub-grown, dry ridges. Palms, on the whole, are not characteristic of this country, and such tall ones as these are definitely uncommon. A few coconuts appear among their fronds.

The palms are tossing about and leaning toward the left because of the heavy north wind, so common in this region, and making the Gulf of Tehuantepec a notably stormy sea. The wind has brought a layer of stratus cloud southward from the Gulf of Mexico, and this has obscured the sky.

28 Isthmus Scene

— The Isthmus of Tehuantepec, along with the low-level routes across Panama and Nicaragua, supplies one of the three easy passages from ocean to ocean. By airline the distance from the Gulf of Mexico to the tidal lagoons near Tehuantepec is 120 miles, and the height of the divide is only 735 feet.

There is no likelihood of anyone's constructing a canal by this route, and in the past the chief project was for a so-called "ship-railroad." In fact, many people think that one was actually constructed, for in a flight of imagination the artist preparing a prospectus for the project drew a picture of a good-sized vessel on a series of freight cars, being hauled across country by a number of engines. This picture was reproduced widely, and naturally gave people the idea that this was what was in existence instead of what was merely projected. An ordinary railroad was constructed across the isthmus by the Mexican government, and finished in 1907.

The view is here northwestward from a point some ten miles east from Tehuantepec. The mountains in the distance rise to about 4000 feet. The stream here is a tidal estuary, which a number of white cranes find greatly to their liking. The richness of the low-growing vegetation makes this good cattle-country, and is the result partly of the lack of drainage of the low-lying plain, and partly of a good rainfall, rather well distributed throughout the year. Because of its location just to the southward of the gap leading from the Gulf, the country around Tehuantepec not only has the ordinary tropical rainy season in the summer months, but also gets rain from northers, especially during December and January. February and March are, in fact, the only dry months in this region. Oaxaca, however, though only 120 miles away by airline, is almost bone-dry for half the year, and gets three-quarters of its rain in the four months from June to September.

The picture was taken on a September morning when this region was still under tropical weather-control. The mottled sky is from moisture drawn in by the sea breeze from the Pacific during the night. Later in the day the powerful sun will transform these stratus clouds into towering cumulus, from which a heavy afternoon shower will probably be released.

If Puente Tlacotepec means "Bridge over the Tlacotepec River," as it should, we have an interesting nomenclatural situation. *Tlaco-* apparently means some kind of plant, and *tepec* certainly means "hill." A stream is thus named for a hill — an unusual, though by no means unparalleled, phenomenon. The suffix *-tepec* is common in this region, as was noted by Thomas Gage in his famous seventeenth-century journey. The five chief towns through which he passed bore that ending.

29 Highway Utilization

— The Mexican — and especially an Indian — believes that highway-use should not be restricted to motor vehicles or even to travel in the broadest sense. Here an Indian — a few miles west of Chiapa de Corzo — finds the smooth and comparatively clean expanse of the highway very convenient for drying his corn. (And good-enough corn it is, too!) The idea, however, is probably not altogether a good one, for on some occasion a trucker or bus-driver is likely to steer right through the middle of the corn, just to show the Indian that highways are not built for agricultural purposes. In fact, to avoid an accident, anyone might have to do the same.

All the way from Chiapa to Comitán is Indian country. The corn-drier may never have been more than a day's walk from the spot where he now stands, and his costume follows an ancient tradition. The white cloth of his blouse and pants may have been machine-woven, but the garments were never thus made up. His broad hat conforms only to local style, and the sandals with the cord passing between the big toe and the one next to it depart from the general fashion of Mexican *huaraches*.

Like most Indians, this one knows a business opportunity when he sees it, and he has just been paid for having his picture taken. In fact, you can see the peso note still clutched in his left hand. Like most Indians of the region, moreover, he goes in for no foolishness about the camera stealing his soul away, and he is only too happy to pose, his face wearing the half-smile so much favored by a man of distinction anywhere, especially just after he has completed a good business-deal.

Not so the small boy who accompanied him! He was definitely camera-shy, and ran to hide behind one of the corn-sacks, thus accounting for its upright posture.

Other details of interest about the man are the strange markings on his left leg, the net carrying-bag he has laid in the gutter, and the water-gourd on the ground just behind his knees.

The stone-work forming the gutter is also of some note. This is all hand-constructed, and would be exorbitantly expensive in the United States. Just beyond the end of the gutter a pile of gravel has been dumped, and has been allowed to spill over onto the highway. If the Indian had laid his corn out just beyond this gravel he would have been in a safer position.

This picture was taken near the end of October, and the dry season had already set in. The leaves have fallen from some of the bushes in the background. The view in this direction shows only undistinguished rolling country, brush-covered, at an altitude of 1000-2000 feet. Looking in the other direction, however, one could see the highway running head-on into the high escarpment of the Chiapas highlands.

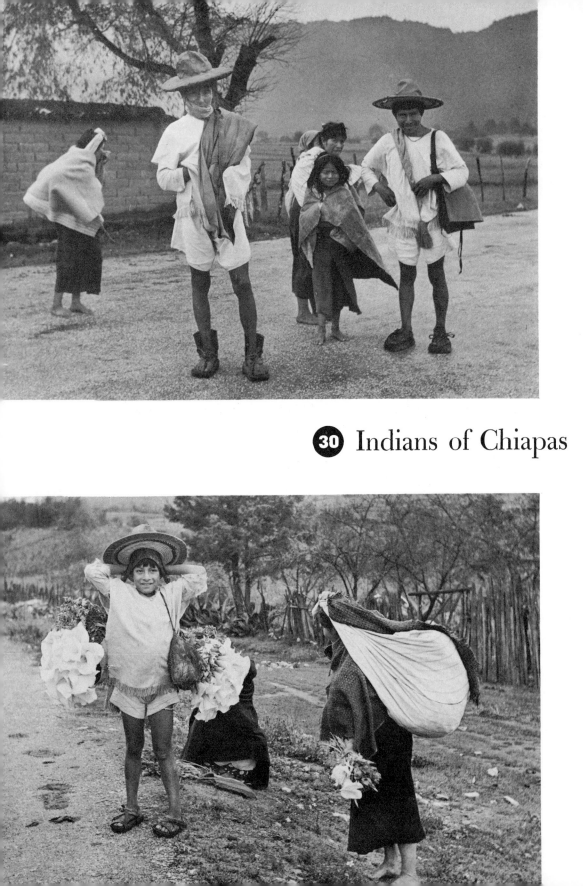

30 Indians of Chiapas

• San Cristóbal is a great center for Indians. They are of different tribes, and differ in their costumes, but with the resemblance that the men are gaily dressed, some of them with bright-colored ribbons on their hats, while the women are drab. At the first coming of the tourists these Indians raised strenuous objections against having their pictures taken. Already, however, most of them have become used to it, and a peso apiece for people in the picture has become a standard compensation, though any good bargainer will naturally try to get more.

Since the morning was misty, the two men (upper picture) had sensibly covered their fine hats and colored ribbons beneath waterproof covers. Their tassels and fringes, however, are still visible. Note the distinctive footwear on the man to the left, with the high backs extending well up the calf.

Having collected his five pesos (babies not counted), this fellow poses self-consciously, and with satisfaction. He feels that he makes a handsome picture. The other, less sophisticated, looks on with interest, and grins.

The girl, barefooted like the women, stands smiling, but with her eyes closed, as if expecting an explosion. Behind her, the woman looks sideways at the camera with a glance that is at least hostile, if not a little malevolent. Suspicion of picture-taking seems to linger with the women. The other one does not even look at the camera, and holds fingers to nose — possibly to prevent her soul escaping and being taken off along with her picture. . . .

As for the boy with the flowers, his mother was so proud of her handsome son that she pushed him in front of the camera without much interest in the money. He himself was very doubtful about the matter at first; possibly he had never been photographed before. He recovered quickly, however, and with the love of posing which is common among the men of this region, he now strikes what seems to him a fine posture — arms behind head — to display himself, his clothes, and his flowers.

Again, the women are taking no chances. The burden-bearer at the right has turned away from the camera; the one in the rear, although actually hidden behind the callas, has squatted down and covered herself completely. Although one woman has a fine hand-woven *rebozo*, its colors are subdued, and she conforms to the general pattern of drabness. She, also, is barefoot.

These pictures were taken a mile from the town of San Cristóbal, about 8.30 in the morning, when the Indians were going in to market.

③① San Cristóbal las Casas

● Founded only a few years after the conquest, capital of Chiapas until late in the nineteenth century, the little town of San Cristóbal las Casas has been known by many names in its history, and still is called either San Cristóbal for St. Christopher, or Las Casas, the latter derived from the saint-like figure of Bartolomé de las Casas, "Apostle to the Indians," first bishop of the diocese.

The town lies between two church-crowned hills, and the view is here from one of them, where the church of San Cristóbal stands, toward the other, which is held by the white-domed shrine of Guadalupe.

The town itself, strikingly white, can be observed between, and thanks to the height of the hill, we can look into the patios of the nearer houses. The view is therefore to be contrasted with that of the street scene in Oaxaca (see Picure 19). Three generally reliable guidebooks that I have examined describe the streets of San Cristóbal as cobblestoned, narrow, and tortuous. Presumably one book may copy from another, but I am a little at a loss to understand how such a three-way and one hundred per cent error could have arisen. Perhaps the original writer merely assumed that such a place would have streets of that kind and so wrote them down without going to see, or else recalled them as what they should have been without remembering what they were. As the picture fully demonstrates, the streets are straight; they are not, for Mexico, particularly narrow; and most of them are smoothly paved.

The large untowered church slightly to the left is the cathedral, notable chiefly for the sculptures on its facade, and suggesting not so much Mexican as Guatemalan architecture — naturally enough, since Chiapas was a part of Guatemala in colonial times.

The large arcaded building just this side of the cathedral is the government palace, and the plaza lies just beyond it.

The heavy clouds are unfortunately too typical of the locality, since the town is at an altitude of 7100 feet, near the top of the mountains, and thus likely to catch rains from either the Pacific or the Atlantic.

The scar on the hills near the middle of the picture has resulted from the passing of people and animals between the town and the hill-villages and the accompanying erosion.

The checkerboard plan for cities, as here seen, is almost universal in Mexico, aside from hill-towns such as Zacatecas and Guanajuato. This devotion of the Spaniards to rectangularity is somewhat curious, since the towns of Spain itself are very irregularly built, and since the Indian towns do not seem to have been remarkable for regularity. Although rectilinear lines are considered a feature of cities in the United States, they did not become popular until after the laying-out of Philadelphia in 1682, and even after that time we find many exceptions, so that the checkerboard pattern is no more characteristic of the United States than of Mexico.

32 Highway Descending

✚ A few miles south of La Trinitaria the highway tumbles over the edge of the plateau, at 5000 feet, and drops rapidly to under 2000 — from pines to palms in half an hour. In doing so, it twists so extremely that one can hardly say which way we are here facing. The picture itself was taken from the roadside, thus indicating still another curve. Actually, the general direction is southwest, and the chief view of the road, to the left, is toward Guatemala.

This is a new road, having been paved since 1950. Nevertheless, it already shows some patching. At the right, the inevitable rainy-season landslide has come down, narrowing the already narrow pavement.

The opening of this road to the border was celebrated with the famous 1950 border-to-border road-race, which started at Ciudad Juárez. This tortuous stretch, as yet unpaved, proved particularly trying to the already tired drivers, and gave some of the more maneuverable European cars an advantage over their unwieldly American rivals. This particular spot, with its view of the hairpin turns, attracted photographers of the event.

In the center of the picture is a characteristic bare, shallow depression, marking a place from which earth was stolen for fills. A cow wanders across it, and several others graze on the farther hillside; in spite of its forbidding aspect, this is cattle-country.

Branching off from the highest curve is the faint trace of wheel-marks, which can be followed along the hillside. This is very likely a "pioneer road," used during the time of the construction of the highway.

In the distance, to the left, appears the far-off tropical lowland. It is here the valley of the Grijalva River, an important stream which rises in the mountains of Guatemala and flows northward to the Gulf of Mexico. A few clearings appear — either cultivated fields or pastures — but most of the country is overgrown.

The farther mountains, at the left, are probably in Guatemala, which is only twenty miles away. Straight ahead, the Pacific Ocean is not more than 90 miles distant, beyond the rampart of mountains. Except for the cover of clouds, the volcanic cone of Tacana (13,417 feet) would probably be in view.

33 Highway Disappearing

✛ This might be called a science-fiction pre-view of what our highways would be like in a year or two if man were quietly removed from the earth. It is a view near the Mexico-Guatemala border.

Since at this time (1955) the highway had not been put through to connect with the road in Guatemala, and since there was no local traffic beyond the town of El Ocotal, there was no need for the Mexican government to expend money in maintaining this section. As a result, the jungle has filled the ditches, and is rapidly encroaching on the pavement from both sides. In the foreground a hardy bush has even forced its way through an unpatched break in the pavement. The approaching dry season will halt this onset of vegetation temporarily, but in a few more years the highway might well be entirely overrun with vines, with reaching branches, and with more bushes sprouting up from cracks in the asphalt.

Back from the line of the highway rise the finely-spreading trees of the tropical forest. The altitude here is about 2500 feet, and growth is luxuriant.

In the distance the cloud-covered mountains rise high and forbidding. These are the Cuchumatanes, and from this view we can appreciate the misgivings of Thomas Gage, when he approached them in 1626, "seeing nothing before me but high and steepy hills and mountains." As so often in Mexico and Guatemala, clearings for cultivation appear high up on the steep mountainsides.

Highest of all, however, are the clouds, pressing down upon the peaks and ridges, as so often in the rainy season, not only seeming to add, but actually adding, further risk to the highway in the higher mountains.

At about the time of the taking of this picture (October 24, 1955) a contract was let for the opening of the highway to connect with the road-head in Guatemala. (See Picture 34.) Work was delayed by a severe rainy season of 1956. In February, 1957, it became possible to "jeep" through between Mexico and Guatemala. In March a few private cases were permitted to make the passage. The present expectation is that the road will be open to traffic at the end of the year. The permanent bridges, however, will probably not be finished until 1959, and during this interval traffic may be occasionally interrupted.

The long record of delays and frustrations associated with the building of the Pan-American Highway makes one a little dubious about any predictions, but this time the prospects are favorable.

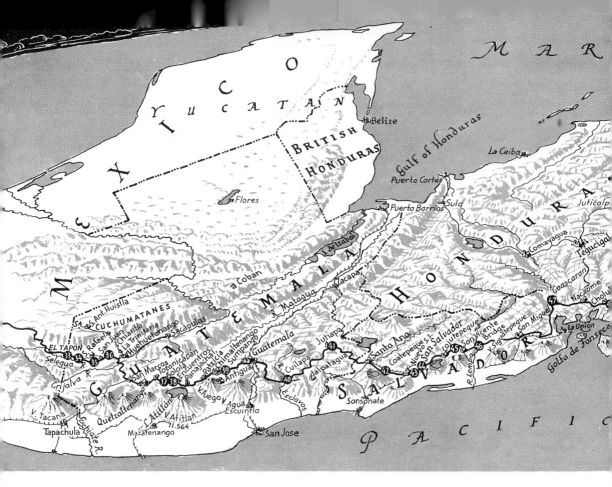

ISTHMUS ROAD

El Tapón and Southward

Surveyed, but unconstructed, for twenty-five miles just south of the Mexican border the "highway" remained not even a road at all for so long that this section came to be known as El Tapón, "the plug." We may hope that this name will be preserved in the future — as a reminder of difficulties and as a link with history.

From El Tapón the highway extends (1956) southward to San Isidro in

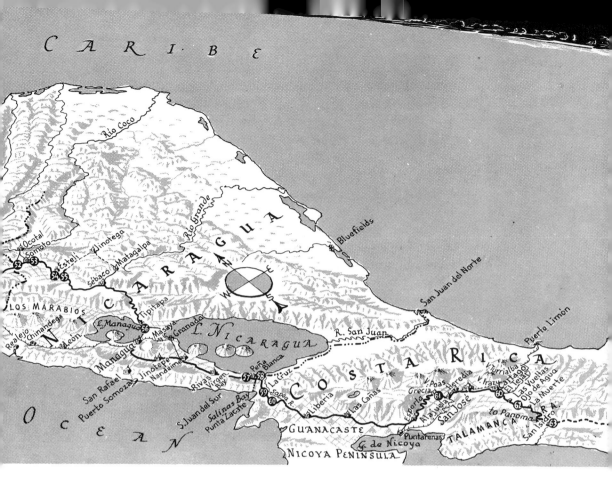

Costa Rica, a distance of 1100 miles. In Guatemala, however, the tourist must follow local roads for many miles, usually at no great distance from the line of proposed construction of the highway, since the highway itself has not yet been built.

By all tests the isthmian section of the road can be considered a unit. Region of extremes and unending variety, split into separate nations — still, Central America in general differs more from Mexico than its own regions and nations differ one from another. The break is not, indeed, sharp.

Northern Mexico is less like Central America than is southern Mexico, and the states of Puebla and Oaxaca are less like Central America than is the border state of Chiapas. This last, indeed, was a part of Guatemala until 1824.

Geographically, this southern section of the highway passes through a region which is primarily an isthmus, and always seems to maintain what may be called an isthmian quality. Just as the English Channel and the Strait of Dover are called "the narrow seas," so the Central American republics might be called "the narrow lands." From the highway, where it crosses the Talamanca Mountains in southern Costa Rica, the tourist can even see the two oceans from one spot.

The isthmus is not, indeed, so narrow that one feels any anxiety about inadvertently driving off either edge of it. Yet, unless I am imagining things, there is a certain cramped quality about it, for all that. Small countries, seem to be reflected in small cities and towns, and even smaller villages. Valleys are cramped in between mountains or between mountains and ocean, and even the mountains, though they are sometimes high, typically go up in neat-appearing volcanic cones.

In fact, the geography of Central America has a kind of two-dimensional simplicity. It can be conceived as three curving but more or less parallel lines — a narrow coastal plain on the Atlantic, a string of mountains up the middle, a narrow coastal plain on the Pacific. The highway alternates between the mountains and the Pacific plain.

In the way of life, also, there is something a little isthmian and cramped. On the highway you do not see goods being transported so much by big roaring trucks as by ox-carts, or even by hand-carts, and on the backs of plodding little men.

Driving southward, the tourist may well think of the road as dividing into well-marked sections. Some of these coincide with national boundaries, but they are more fundamentally determined by differences in altitude, terrain, climate, and even soil. Indeed, were not the national boundaries themselves to some extent determined by these more fundamental features? In all, eight sections of highway may be noted.

1) *The Highlands of Guatemala.* From El Tapón the first section extends to Guatemala City and a little south of it — a matter of 250 miles.

These are the Highlands of Guatemala. No region of the continent more aptly deserves the title of the Switzerland of America. It is small, mountainous, highly scenic, and even maintains the analogy by having excellent hotels. It offers antiquities, native inhabitants in an amazing variety of rainbow-hued costumes, fiestas, bargains in native handicrafts for the shopper, and endless targets for the photographer. In short, it is a tourist's paradise, and the most colorful stretch of highway to be encountered on the north-south road.

2) *Eastern Guatemala.* Beyond Guatemala City the highway descends, and enters the region that we may merely call Eastern Guatemala. Here, for a hundred miles, the country can only be described as undistinguished. There are no more gaily clad Indians along the road, but only ordinary *Ladinos.* As a Guatemalan described this section to me, in words neither complimentary to it or to the inhabitants of one of our states, "This is our Okie country." The soil is rocky and poor, so that the natural growth is scrubby and only small areas are under cultivation. Towns and villages, also, are poor, and the whole countryside is thinly inhabited.

3) *The Salvador Plateau.* As it crosses the border and leaves Guatemala behind, the highway enters what we may call the Salvador Plateau. This extends most of the way across that country, a distance of about one-hundred-fifty miles. It is a rich and productive area, most of it between two and three thousand feet above sea-level. This is a scenic region, with volcanoes standing up picturesquely and many fine vistas of highly cultivated valleys.

4) *Tropical-Scrub Country.* Near San Miguel the highway drops to the coastal plain, and for almost a hundred miles, continues nearly at sea level — in Salvador and in Honduras. This region resembles Eastern Guatemala, but is even less scenic, and is likely to be extremely hot. There is little cultivation, and the vegetation is mostly of that sort which can be most aptly described as "tropical scrub." Yet, lacking though it may be in the attractions, this stretch of lowland has its own points of interest. The tourist from the north here sees what he will call the "real tropics." Actually there are about as many different kinds of "real tropics" as there are of pigeons, but this stretch is certainly one of them.

5) *Frontier Country.* Beyond the great Choluteca Bridge the highway begins to rise steadily, and soon crosses the Continental Divide at an eleva-

tion of 3776 feet. Almost to Sébaco, for more than a hundred miles, it passes through what we may call Frontier Country. This is a hilly plateau region, extending from Honduras into Nicaragua, ranging between 3000 and 4000 feet in altitude. There are few towns, and those small. The scenery is moderately varied, but not spectacular. Here, as in the preceding section, the tourist will be chiefly interested in observing the primitive ways of life still existing in this region, which was completely isolated until the very recent punching-through of the highway. I have called this Frontier Country, not because it lies along the boundary of two nations, but because it is largely undeveloped and yet seems to be developing and to have the capacity for much future growth.

6) *Deep Tropics.* Some miles before reaching Sébaco, the highway descends from the hills. The tourist will note a curious feeling of having returned to civilization at seeing even ox-carts, after the primitive pack-trains which he may have passed in the hill country. This next section, extending 165 miles to the southern border of Nicaragua, we may call the "deep tropics." Except for the considerable bump which the highway crosses south of Managua, the altitude is everywhere close to sea-level, and there is no such thing as cold or even cool weather. In most of the hotels of Managua the faucets run only one kind of water — luke-warm.

For sheer variety and novelty the tourist will find this stretch rating close to the top. It has its scenery — volcanic cones, and far-reaching lakes. Along it he can observe cattle ranges, field crops, and coffee plantations. The natural vegetation varies from grassland and tropical scrub to jungle and rain-forest such as one would expect on the banks of the Amazon. As for modes of human habitation, one can see everything from the sophisticated suburban developments around Managua, to the primitive huts along the shores of Lake Nicaragua.

7) *Guanacaste.* Immediately on crossing into Costa Rica, the highway enters a section which may merely be called by the name of the province through which it passes. Guanacaste — once joined to Nicaragua, but a part of Costa Rica since 1824 — offers a passageway for the road as far as Esparta. There are some hills to be crossed, and some views — to the east, of the Guanacaste Mountains; to the west, of the ocean. On the whole, however, this is a somewhat monotonous country, thinly inhabited, overgrown with "dry" tropical forest, chiefly devoted to cattle-raising.

8) *Highlands of Costa Rica.* At Esparta, the highway enters the mountains. From this point to San Isidro, the tourist passes across the highlands of Costa Rica, crossing two ranges of high mountains, and the famous Meseta Central which lies between them. At an altitude of 10,932 the road attains its highest point at the Cerro de la Muerte, "the hill of death," supposed to have been so-called in the "old days" because of the hardships encountered on the trail at this point. Almost everywhere along this 140-mile section the scenery is beautiful; in many places, spectacularly magnificent.

Beyond San Isidro — at the time of writing, as yet unpenetrated by a road — the jungles of southern Costa Rica extend for 130 miles to the border of Panama.

The story of the Isthmus Road, if records were available, could undoubtedly be carried far back into pre-Columbian times. The northern part of Central America was one of the great areas of ancient civilization, as its many ruins still testify. Here, however, as in Mexico, wheeled vehicles and beasts of burden were lacking, and so there was no need for anything better than good foot-trails.

Highly exceptional, perhaps dictated more for religious than for everyday ends, were the roads radiating from the Mayan city of Coba in Yucatan. One of these was 62 miles long, and even in its remains resembles a Roman road in its straightness and in its solid stone construction. A stone road-roller, used in the construction-work, has been found close beside the road.

Foot trails can be established with comparatively little labor, and so there are likely to be many of them in any well-inhabited and not too difficult primitive country. Even now, the highlands of Guatemala, back from the automobile roads, have many trails, some of them worn deep by long-continued travel.

A network of trails thus probably existed in the more inhabited parts of ancient Central America. Some were used only by local villagers; others, by the merchants on their long-distance journeys. As in southern Mexico one trail would be favored in the wet season; another, in the dry.

Since the passage of time does not change the easiest passes or the best stream-crossings and since a straight line remains the shortest distance between two given points, there is every likelihood that the Spaniards merely took over the principal Indian trail for their own north-south road. As in Mexico, the *conquistadores* — whether Alvarado in Guatemala or Gil Gonzales in Nicaragua — found the trails passable in the dry season. The latter, indeed, got into trouble when he was overtaken by the rains, and had to build boats and get his forces back to the seacoast by river.

After the Conquest, the Spaniards presumably improved the trails some- what, for the passage of mounted men, pack-mules, and artillery. But the difficulties of long-distance transport remained great. During the six-month rainy season movement was almost impossible. The beginning of every dry season found the trails washed out and in poor condition, and even though streams became fordable and mud dried up with the ceasing of the rains, mountains and jungles still presented barriers. Naturally, therefore, the Spaniards adopted the simpler process of transporting themselves and their goods down to the nearest seaport and then taking ship for a coastwise voyage.

Only toward the end of the sixteenth century did this system begin to break down. Various reasons are presented for this failure of the merchant marine — piracy, restrictive laws, a general decline of enterprise. One factor was certainly the appearance of English ships in the Pacific. First it was Drake in 1579 and then Cavendish in 1587 — capturing and sinking ships, and plundering towns. This was a terrific shock to the Spaniards' complacency, and they reacted violently. When Hawkins tried the same trick in 1594, he found a Spanish fleet waiting for him, and was captured before he ever got north of Chile. But besides getting their fleet ready, the Spaniards also did just as the United States did in 1942 when the Germans and Japanese menaced the sea-lanes, that is, they set out to establish an overland route. At least, the fact is sure that the Spaniards began to develop the north-south road at this time.

Two notable achievements, in fact, fall within one decade. In 1592 the great Esclavos Bridge (see Picture 40) was completed, thus assuring the passage of a dangerous stream which could often be neither forded nor fer- ried. Also, in 1601, a mule-trail was opened up through the difficult country of mountains and jungle between Cartago in Costa Rica and Chiriquí in what is now Panama.

Of this latter achievement only a few details can be supplied. We know that the trail was put through by Gonzalo Vásquez de Coronado, Acting

Governor of Costa Rica, in the early months of the year, that is, in the dry season. Since he seems to have encountered no difficulties other than the natural ones of terrain, we may assume that he followed some kind of Indian path, and merely improved this for the passage of pack-trains. It is a pleasure, however, to be able at least to record of Vásquez himself that he is reported to have been a very popular person, especially with his soldiers, because of his being very liberal with his money.

In 1598, just three years earlier, Oñate had opened the road to New Mexico in the north; now it was opened to the south. Thus in 1601 a man could ride horseback on an established trail, clear from the Rio Grande to Panama!

As to where the Isthmus Road went and what it was like, in the early seventeenth century, we can again call upon Thomas Gage for testimony.

In September, 1626, that far-wandered Englishman crossed the line of the present Mexico-Guatemala border, on mule-back, at a point probably about fifteen miles to the north of where the highway now crosses. His trail kept to the north, passing through San Martín, and going close to Chiantla. Then, it went east to Sacapulas, and then south and east, not returning to the line of the highway until Chimaltenango. Thence Gage proceeded the short distance to the Guatemala City of his day, that is, the present Antigua.

Since Gage followed this route and since he was always a comfort-loving and somewhat timorous traveler, we can only suppose that this was the main wet-season route at that time. The dry-season route, however, must have gone from Antigua to Quezaltenango, and there was undoubtedly a trail between Quezaltenango and Huehuetenango, so that the general line of the highway was probably a mule-trail in Gage's time.

Gage had set out upon this part of his journey with much trepidation, having heard of rough mountains and uninhabited wastes. He was, however, agreeably surprised: "Though the Mountains seemed high afar off, yet as I traveled on, I found the way lie between them very easy and passable." Again he noted: "The further I went, the better and more open I found the Road," even though it was the rainy season and he suffered from showers and mud. Moreover, he now and then met pack-trains of mules.

Having arrived at Antigua, Gage settled down, and in that city and its vicinity, he remained for ten years. He served for three years as Reader of

Arts at a convent school, which he called "the university." Then, he became the parish priest in the near-by town of Petapa. He lived there very comfortably indeed, and gradually accumulated a sizeable sum from his fees and from "gifts" from the Indians. (Later, having renounced Catholicism, he vented his spleen against such priestly corruption.)

Desiring to return home to England with his nest-egg, Gage deserted a second time, and fled away, having sent his valuables ahead in some chests under the charge of an Indian servant. The direct route toward Europe would have led him across to the Atlantic coast, but he did not dare to go that way for fear of being apprehended as a recreant priest. Thus, a second time, his necessity is our profit, since he was forced to follow the road southward.

On January 7, 1637, at midnight, he surreptitiously left Petapa, on muleback, accompanied by a loyal "blackamoor." Making every effort to avoid meeting anyone who would recognize him, he traveled as rapidly as possible through the darkness. From about daybreak he must have been following the line of the present highway, or close to it. Sometime in the course of the day, having already covered about thirty miles, he came to the Esclavos River, with its massive bridge, already nearly half a century old. There he stopped only long enough "to drink a cup of chocolate and to bait our mules." (Whenever Gage decided to run away, he seems to have gone into panic, and he took no chances of being overtaken.)

Soon after leaving the Esclavos, the line of his road left that of the present highway, and headed southeast. Passing probably through Jalpatagua, Gage continued his breakneck flight until toward evening he arrived at Ahuachapán. At this point, he had traveled, muleback and almost without resting, a distance of at least sixty miles. Even so, he halted only until midnight, and then rode thirteen miles farther to breakfast at Chalchuapa. Following this route, he must have returned to the line of the highway at Santa Ana.

Not wishing to pass through San Salvador in the daylight, he delayed, and went through the city in the evening. He continued all night, apparently along the line of the highway, and about daybreak came to the Lempa River. Having been ferried across, he now breathed easier, believing that he had put enough distance between himself and the authorities in Guatemala.

The next day he arrived at San Miguel, where he was faced with the usual alternative of travelers in that direction. Should he take boat and cross the Gulf of Fonseca, or should he follow the trail through Nacaome? The latter would be a three-day journey, about a hundred miles, to Realejo on the coast of Nicaragua. Gage sent his Indian with the baggage by land, a good evidence of the safety of the roads. He himself went down to the gulf, and embarked. Setting sail on the afternoon of what must have been January 12, he landed at La Vieja, at eight the next morning.

Being rejoined by the Indian, Gage went on through Realejo and Leon, to Granada. In so doing he must have come to the line of the present highway at Managua, and he probably followed along it for a few miles. He makes no mention of Managua, however, which at that time was an insignificant village. Halting at Granada, Gage tried to get a passage in one of the vessels which made their way across Lake Nicaragua and down the San Juan River to the Caribbean.

While waiting, he made note of the many mule-trains arriving from the north. There was a busy trade in indigo, cochineal, and sugar, from Honduras, Salvador, and even from the farther-off Guatemala. One whole pack-train arrived with silver, the King's share from the mines. Gage recorded the arrival of six large pack-trains, at least three hundred mules, in a single day. Undoubtedly the main road, which Gage himself had traveled except for his brief voyage, was open and easy.

There was a particular reason for the heavy traffic of this year. Dutch and English pirates were cruising off the ports of Guatemala and Honduras, and so the Spaniards were attempting to avoid this danger by using the Nicaragua route. The pirates, however, soon shifted their operations southward. The magistrates at Granada therefore canceled the sailing of all ships, and Gage was frustrated. Again to our advantage, he decided to continue by land.

Setting out in company with three Spaniards and an Indian guide, he went south from Granada. On the second and third days they followed close along Lake Nicaragua, as the highway now goes.

At one point the travelers had an adventure, though we must take this story with a grain of salt, as with Gage's tale of nearly being blown off the mountains into the Pacific Ocean near Tehuantepec. They were passing, it seems, some pool or lagoon near the lake and barely noticed what seemed to be a tree-trunk afloat in it. But this suddenly transformed itself into a monstrous crocodile, which came rushing out to seize some man or mule. The travelers set spur to their mounts, but the beast was too fast and was overhauling them. One of the Spaniards cried out "to turn on another side, and so to circumflex our way." Thus dodging, like hares before a hound, they escaped. Gage, still a priest even if a recreant, adds sententiously:

> By this experience we came to know the nature and quality of that beast, whose greatness of body is no hindrance to run forward as swift as a Mule; but otherwise, as the Elephant once laid down is troubled to get up, so this monster is heavy and stiff, and therefore much troubled to turn and wind about his body.

Unfortunately that very reference to the elephant adds to our incredulity, for that story is one of the commonest in medieval animal-lore. As for escaping a crocodile by dodging, that is another ancient story.

Gage and his companions continued on, and after leaving the lake, came to "rough and craggy ways," just as the highway now does south of the Costa Rica border. Like many recent travelers, Gage found Guanacaste a dull place, deserving no special comment. In all probability he followed close to the line of the highway, and his comment runs: "many mountains and desert places, where we lay sometimes two nights together, either in Woods or open fields." This having to sleep out was not to Gage's liking; in spite of all his traveling in rough places, he was always as anxious as a cat for comfort.

From Cartago, Gage went to the east coast, took ship, was robbed by pirates, and found himself forced to return to Cartago. He debated continuing his land-journey with a train of "some two or three hundred mules, unsaddled and unloaden," which were being driven to Panama for sale. His mention of this train is proof that Vásquez's trail was still open. The trade, however, was precariously maintained, as Gage makes clear in a comment:

> This is the yearly and only trading by land, which Guatemala, Camayagua [Honduras], and Nicaragua hath with Panama over that narrow Isthmus lying between the North and South sea, which is very dangerous by reason of the craggy ways, rocks and mountains, but more especially, by reason of many heathens, barbarians and savage people.

At this point we must take leave of Thomas Gage, only to add that he got safe home at last — to shift his church without shifting his character, and to continue as a Protestant in practices as unsavory as those he had followed when a Catholic.

In general, from Gage's account, we can picture the Isthmus Road as a well-established and well-traveled pack-trail. Doubtless ox-carts were used on it in the level sections, particularly near towns, but Gage makes no mention of them. His failure to record much about the condition of the road may be taken as an indication that it offered no special difficulties and was what would have been expected at that time. He was traveling in the dry season, when the small rivers would have been easily fordable. He crossed the Esclavos by its famous bridge; the Lempa, by ferry. The use of two ferry boats at this point indicates a considerable volume of traffic.

By and large, crude though the trail may have been, it was probably as good as most of the contemporary roads in Europe. Even in Gage's native England, goods were still transported largely by pack-train.

As to route, Gage followed that of the present highway for a short distance near the Esclavos River in Guatemala. He struck it again near Santa Ana in Salvador, and followed it until he took boat. If he had continued by land, he would have kept close to the present highway clear to Choluteca. He crossed it near Managua, came to it again in the vicinity of Nandaime in southern Nicaragua, and thence followed it clear to Cartago. Thus the routes of the old and new roads, from the vicinity of Guatemala City to Cartago, are roughly the same for more than half the distance. From Cartago to Panama, moreover, the evidence available indicates that the route of the highway (and the proposed highway) keeps generally close to that of the colonial trail.

In this connection an interesting fact is to be noted. When the two roads diverge, the route followed by the old one is generally better — shorter, and less mountainous. (See Picture 51.)

As the decades ran on to pile up into the centuries, the Isthmus Road changed little, either in route or in condition. If anything, it deteriorated, as traffic over it declined and its maintenance became less important. For, in Central America as elsewhere in the Spanish colonies, the vigorous prosperity of the early seventeenth century soon slumped into depression and stagnation.

There were special reasons, moreover, for the decline of the road. By 1700 piracy had been brought under control, and there was no longer any economic reason for transporting goods such great distances by land. The different regions though politically one, were oriented, not lengthwise, but crosswise on the isthmus. Each district developed special customs, interests, and prejudices. With independence, separatism triumphed over union, a misfortune which the English colonies also barely managed to escape. After independence, cultural isolation and the cross-isthmus point of view continued. Even now, a well-to-do Guatemalan is likely to have closer business relationships with New York than with San Salvador, and to know Paris better than he knows Managua or San José. Naturally, therefore, the road of Gage's travels, which was definitely a through route, broke into segments, serving local interests. It became of less importance than the short roads running down from each city to the nearest seaport.

But to see what it was really like, we can follow a nineteenth-century traveler along it.

Let us call as witness John L. Stephens, aged thirty-five, vigorous in body and inquisitive in mind, already known as "the American traveler." In February, 1840, he found himself in Costa Rica, where he had arrived by a circuitous route which need not concern us. His situation, however, was an embarrassing one. He was a diplomat, bearing a commission from President Van Buren, and trying to find the government to which he was accredited. But the briefly united Central America had by this time split into warring and revolutionary sections, and Stephens quested about in vain from the Dan of Guatemala to the Beersheba of Costa Rica.

Having gone as far south as Cartago, he reversed himself, still seeking the will-o'-the-wisp of a Central American government. From San José he left for Guatemala on the morning of February 13. Never more happy than when setting out, he expressed himself as pleased with the lightness of his baggage and the spirit of his mules, and thus he looked his journey of 1200 miles "boldly in the face."

Clear to Guatemala City the road seems to have followed almost precisely the same route that Gage had followed two centuries previously. In fact, we can imagine the Presidential envoy brushing his stirrup-leathers against those same tree trunks past which the fugitive friar had ridden when they were saplings. Like Gage, Stephens crossed the Gulf of Fonseca, though he embarked and disembarked at different points. In eastern Salvador he went by way of Sonsonate instead of by Chalchuapa — if anyone wishes to be interested in such a detail. Like everyone else in more than three and a half centuries — including me, in 1955 — he crossed the Esclavos bridge, which he noted as "the greatest structure in Central America."

As for the condition of the road, the chief change to be noted is its segmentation. In Gage's time it seems to have been essentially a through route, a good mule-trail everywhere, not much better than that anywhere. In the mountains and across the many thinly inhabited stretches, Stephens found the road no better than it had been in Gage's time, and perhaps worse. At least, he makes many derogatory remarks about it, but this may be merely because a nineteenth-century traveler expected something better than a seventeenth-century one did. But certainly Stephens's occasional comments do not suggest the well-traveled trail of earlier years. Just north of Esparta, in the lowland of Guanacaste, he noted, that the trees were so close as to darken the road, "and the branches so low that it was necessary to keep the head constantly bent to avoid hitting them." Close to Managua, a large rock had rolled down, and the road had merely been detoured around. There was apparently no regular service of maintenance, and Stephens wrote that the rock "probably blocks up the road still." Continuing northward, he crossed the Lempa River, as Gage had done, by a ferry. The boat was large enough to carry sixteen mules and as many people, but apparently there was only one boat, not two, as in Gage's time. Still farther north, Stephens encountered extremely primitive conditions; after crossing the Esclavos bridge he found the main road so little traveled that it was almost indistinguishable from the local trails running off from it, and he was fearful of losing his way.

On the other hand, in the vicinity of towns and throughout the more thickly inhabited regions, the trail of Gage's time had been transformed into a road for the passage of ox-carts and other wheeled vehicles. Between Cartago and San José, for instance, much of the way was "well-paved," doubtless with stone, and was set off by fences. Near Rivas, Stephens found the road "about ten feet wide, straight, and shaded by the noblest trees in the Nicaragua forests."

Stephens made his journey in the full dry season; otherwise, he probably could not have made it at all. Many of the streams would have been unfordable, and in many places the mud would have bogged the mules down. Some indication of what travel was like during the rains may be gathered from Stephens's experiences on what he called, perhaps with some sarcasm, "the great high road" into Guatemala City from the east. This was actually, at the time, a much more traveled road than the north-and-south one along the isthmus. Nevertheless Stephens describes the mules as constantly fetlock-deep in mud, and sometimes wallowing through puddles up to their bellies. Descending a mountain, the trail became "a narrow gulley, worn by the tracks of mules and the rushing of mountain torrents so deep that the sides were higher than our heads, and so narrow that we could barely pass through without touching." Time and again, mules stuck in the mud, even though they were only half-loaded. "We were dragged through mudholes," Stephens continues, "squeezed in gulleys, knocked against trees, and tumbled over roots." The road, in fact, was barely passable, and sometimes, he adds, was not passable at all.

Stephens's route from Guatemala City to the Mexican border is of particular interest, for here he did not retrace Gage's route, but kept fairly close to the present highway.

He set out on April 7, just as the rains were beginning. He passed through Sololá, and Totonicapán, to arrive at Quezaltenango; then he went northward, through Aguascalientes to Huehuetenango. He then ascended a mountain-trail northward, and that night slept at a poor hut near the top of the pass. Next day he went on, down the pass, through Todos Santos to San Martín. On the third day from Huehuetenango, winding about through ravines and over bridges he passed through Petatán, barely escaped a brush fire, and reached San Antonio Huista. He had by this time descended from the mountains, and was at an altitude of about three thousand feet. The next morning, following a more northerly course, descending into narrow river valleys only to climb out again, he came at last to the Lagartero River. A broken bridge, carried away by high water seven years before, stood there as a testimony to the continuing deterioration of the road. From that point Stephens continued to the ruined town of Conata, another testimony to the desolation which had fallen upon the region. After spending a night in the open, he went on through a village, where he saw people for the first time since leaving San Antonio Huista. Thence to Comitán was an easy ride of four hours.

As far as can be gathered from Stephens's account, all the road from Guatemala City to Comitán was nowhere better than a rough mule-trail. He mentions no wheeled vehicles, and indeed these highlands still remain a region where goods are transported by animal-back or man-back.

Before reaching Quetzaltenango he encountered a certain amount of traffic, at one point having to pass a great train of mules — five hundred, he estimated — laden with wheat and textiles for Guatemala City, doubtless from the rich fields and busy hand-looms of Quetzaltenango.

His comments on the road indicate that it was not good, even by mule-trail standards. Here it was "very steep;" there, "exceedingly bad." At one point he "looked down into a frightful abyss two or three thousand feet deep." At another place he spent three hours and a half making six miles. Again there is a mention of a descent "very steep and muddy," where the mountain-wise mules sometimes merely placed their feet and slid down.

Near Huehuetenango, the road was "broken and stony, and the track scarcely perceptible." Gullies and deep ravines intersected it, and across one of these "by way of bridge, lay the trunks of two gigantic pines." One of the pack-mules slipped off the logs, but fortunately at the very beginning of the passage, so that it fell among some bushes and was uninjured. The trail through the empty frontier country beyond Huehuetenango seems to have been less difficult than the more traveled road which he traversed before reaching that point.

The middle of the nineteenth century, with the discovery of gold in California and the intensified need for communications between the east and west coasts of the United States, saw the establishment of the trans-Nicaragua route, and the building of the first good modern road in Central America. This ran from Virgen Bay on Lake Nicaragua across to San Juan del Sur on the Pacific, a distance of only ten miles. It was a "fine plank road," such construction then being considered the last word. With the completion of the Panama railway in 1855, the Nicaragua route lost most of its importance, and in that tropical climate the plank road soon rotted away. In any case, it was a symbol that in the middle of the century the chief interest was still in cross-wise transportation. Central America was conceived, not as a pathway connecting two continents, but as a barrier separating two oceans.

In the later part of the nineteenth century the idea of an inter-continental railway was born and flourished. A proposal sprang from the fertile brain of the famous Hinton R. Helper, a well-hated man in the ante-bellum South because of his *Impending Crisis*. On one occasion he was making a voyage to Buenos Aires. As the weeks passed (fourteen of them) he grew so tired of looking at water that he began to think of how much time he could save if there were a railroad.

Helper had vast energy, a long memory, and some wealth. In 1879 he began to advocate the railroad actively, and put up $5000 for prizes to be awarded for the best essays and poems on the subject. This shows incidentally, the high regard held for poetry in those days. The winner of the $1000 award in that department was an engineer and his 154 five-line stanzas certainly deserve the prize as an example of what might be called "engineering-poetry." The statements as precise as the design for a bridge; the rhymes, as unvarying as a piston-stroke; the stanzas, constructed on the principle of interchangeable parts. Even as the risk of digression, a specimen should be quoted:

> *And there in winter-time,*
> *By fragrant ways along the leafy Isthmus,*
> *The invalid shall seek a milder clime*
> *And find it where the showy Flower of Christmas*
> *Is blooming while our fields are white with rime.*

Helper's plan was simplicity itself. It called for "a longitudinal midland double-track steel railroad," due north-and-south, across the United States from Dakota to Texas; then, from where that line struck the Rio Grande, on "a bee-line" to Mexico City; then, through Central America as nearly midland as possible. It was to pass east of the Andes, "felling the forests and furrowing up the surfaces" of the various countries, until it arrived in Argentina. Monarchical Brazil, however, was to be by-passed, as unworthy of participation.

Mad as all this seems, Helper himself was by no means mad. He memorialized Congress, agitated generally, and accomplished a good deal. By Congressional action an Intercontinental Railway Commission operated from 1890 to 1898, investigated routes, and published a far-from-negligible report.

Some Central American railroads were constructed as thus projected, and eventually it became possible to travel by rail all the way from the United States to La Unión in Salvador, almost at the Honduras border. If Henry Ford and some others had not changed the course of history, a line would probably be in existence, clear to the Canal. Most railroads in Central America, however, were built to connect the inland regions with the nearest seaport, and they thus show the crosswise state of mind still predominating.

As for the automobile, its influence was very late in becoming of importance in Central America, an economically backward and physically rugged region. Even though Costa Rica was one of the more advanced of the republics, a paragraph summarizing its transportation in 1927 made no mention of automotive facilities at all. This, however, was about the end, and isthmian nostrils were not much longer destined to remain unpuckered by the smell of gasoline fumes. Plans for a through road were already being formulated. The long and fluctuating and often discouraging history of the attempt to construct the Pan-American Highway has already been told.

34 El Tapón

— This is the end of the road, seen from the Guatemala side, looking northward, in October, 1955. Work is already under way in the canyon ahead, and the power-shovel of an American road-building company is in view.

The picture illustrates the precipitous nature of the Selegua River gorge, and the consequent difficulties of road-building that have delayed completion. No early route of travel passed through this gorge; Gage, Stephens, and others kept to the north (right) on trails that crossed over the mountains.

At the left the cliff has already been blasted away to a height of a hundred feet or more, merely to allow the passage of a narrow "pioneer road." Much more work will have to be done before a highway of standard width can be accommodated. Below the road these loose rocks, some of them very large, have been dumped into the gorge, thus further restricting the flow of the river. Through this narrow passage the Selegua, coffee-with-cream color and running high because of recent rains, swirls downward on its long course to join the Grijalva, and eventually to contribute its waters to the Gulf of Mexico.

The altitude here is about 5000 feet, with the mountains rising several thousand feet higher. The natural vegetation is thorn-scrub at lower altitudes, changing to pines higher up. Long-continued attempts at farming, however, have changed the aspect of the landscape. Fields, some of them incredibly steep, hang on the mountainsides. Some of these are still cultivated in corn; others have been abandoned, probably because of erosion, and now show only as areas of thinner growth. In spite of their steepness, these fields are plowed by oxen. The volcanic soils of these Guatemalan highlands are highly fertile, and do not erode easily. Still, no field can last long on such hillsides, and the yellow-brown river is thus easily explainable.

The story among workers on the highway was that several fields had slid down into the roadway as the result of blasting. I see no reason why this should not be literally true.

The tops of the farther mountains are covered with cloud. The frequency of this phenomenon during the rainy season furnished an additional motive for taking the highway through the gorge at lower altitude. The dense mountain-top fogs form a real hazard for the motorist in Central America, especially at night.

35 Highland Village

— Twenty miles toward Mexico from Huehuetenango, high on the mountainside above the Selegua River, at an altitude of about 7000 feet, stands the primitive and "unspoiled" Guatemalan village of San Rafael. Luckily the new highway will by-pass it, thus providing some chance that it will not be too quickly altered by sudden influx of tourists.

This is a brilliant morning at 9.30, with only a few puff-ball clouds in the sky. It is a Sunday, and the villagers are holding their market in front of church, where many of them are standing about.

The church itself is typically Guatemalan — low-built, small and unassuming, shining white. Its three surmounting crosses tip informally, each at its own angle.

Even in this well-wooded area tile is the usual roof-covering. No one seems to have the art of making shingles, and thatch is reserved for the low-country. The house at the right, however, shows a liberal use of wood. Except in such mountain country as this, the upright post would be of brick or stone.

The old man with his staff, who is approaching, is not wearing one of the gay native costumes, though these are common in this region. Most people in the highlands object to having their pictures taken; having found himself the center of one, this old fellow contented himself with collecting a small payment.

Even such an isolated village as this does not altogether escape modern commercialism, as is evidenced by the advertisement for a headache pill posted on the house.

The background shows typical highland country — pine-covered mountains, and occasional cleared fields.

The rough and narrow road on which the old man is approaching is not only the chief street of the village but was also the highway in 1955.

**36** Burden Bearers

● Horse, mule, burro, and ox, as domestic animals, came to North America after the Conquest. In regions dominated by Indian tradition, these innovations have never been wholly accepted, and much of the freight moves by man-back.

The happy-looking Indian (upper right) sat by the side of the road a few miles north of Huehuetenango, to which town he was going with his pots. He differed from most of the Guatemalans of that area in having no objection to being photographed.

He has a fine Indian face, with a good drooping mustache. His excellent teeth, again typical, shine out brightly. His baldness seems to be caused chiefly by the friction of his tump-line, which he has thrown off while sitting down, so that it rests just back of his head. His load is loosely packed in a net, and he has a staff to aid him in walking. . . .

In contrast, the two little Indians (upper left) produce an effect of poverty, over-work, oppression, and even fear. They are of the border-country of Chiapas in Mexico, which is largely Guatemalan in custom. They are carrying their overwhelming loads of charcoal into the near-by village of La Trinitaria. When I asked to take the picture, they merely submitted, obviously not feeling that they could refuse anything to a man who rode in an automobile. Their eyes peer out more in apprehension than in wonder. The peso (worth seven cents) that I gave them afterwards came as a surprise, but it undoubtedly represented a sum of importance to them. They wear the local costume, but so grimy and worn as scarcely to be picturesque. From the man's neck is suspended a bag to be used in carrying purchases home. . . .

The four men with their tremendous loads of pots I caught, just before sunrise, at the village of Panajachal. They are headed toward Guatemala City, which is probably their destination, though it is sixty miles off, and will require three days' walking. This is what their ancestors have done through many generations. Now, however, there are some ironies in the situation, for they are walking upon a good road, and beneath a modern power-line. A man's load in Guatemala is rated at 150 pounds, and these four would seem to be up to that standard. In keeping with the long journey that they are to make, their loads are packed on carrying-devices, which look like small tables. A patch of colorful native costume shows, just below the "table-top."

37 Cold Country

— Central America, even more than Mexico, lies so close to the equator that climate — temperature, in particular — is determined not so much by latitude as by altitude. General usage distinguishes the hot country (Tierra Caliente) up to 3000 feet, the temperate country (Tierra Templada) between 3000 and 7000 feet, and the cold country (Tierra Fria) above 7000 feet. There is no sharp line of demarcation, and the zones shade into one another.

By any rating, the country here shown would have to be rated as cold, since it lies at an altitude of about 10,500 feet, and is close to the highest point reached by the highway in Guatemala. The location is about five miles northwest of Los Encuentros. The road here is merely a local Guatemalan one, not graded up to Pan-American standards. In fact, the building of the highway will necessitate a relocation here, and the new road will pass somewhat to the south, through similar country.

Altitude is indicated by the growth of conifers, mostly pines. The open grassy spaces show that this is close to timber-line. Trees once displaced by lumbering or fire can only with difficulty re-establish themselves at this height.

The makeshift and half-ruined hut is of interest as showing primitive methods of construction. It is loosely built of poles, and has been originally thatched with straw. Lacking a chimney and tight walls, it is quite unsuited to its location; it resembles the huts of the tropical lowlands, and suggests a makeshift adaptation. Possibly it was constructed as a temporary protection for workmen when the road was being built, or else it was originally erected as a shelter for benighted travelers.

This road is not paved; the surface has been patched with broken stone, and is moderately rough. The curve is too sharp for safety, and the pile of rock carelessly allowed to spill onto the highway offers another hazard, as well as obstructing drainage. The three stakes set along the side of the road also seem to offer more of danger than of safety.

The sharp and long shadows of the stakes indicate that the picture was taken on a bright sunny morning, about eight o'clock.

 Volcanoes

● In his classic description of Central America, John L. Stephens wrote that the country "bristles with volcanic cones." In their arrangement they might even be compared to a picket-fence, extending along the western side of the high country and separating it from the coastal plain.

Here, for instance, at a point about five miles south of Los Encuentros, we look out southward from an altitude of about 9000 feet across high country toward the even higher peaks. At the left, in almost perfect symmetry, Atitlán rises to a height of 11,564; at the right, the less impressive San Pedro attains 9920. Actually another volcano is in view, since Toliman (about 10,750 feet) rises immediately in front of Atitlán, but is blotted out against the silhouette of its larger neighbor. These mountains rise from the shore of beautiful Lake Atitlán. A distant arm of the lake (or perhaps the morning mist covering its surface) can be seen about halfway between the two peaks. Mist from the lake also produces a slight halo around the base of the larger cone.

The peak of Atitlán is about fifteen miles distant. Seen thus from the highlands, it displays only about half of its real height. From the other direction it towers up from almost sea-level, rising from the edge of the coastal plain. The peak looks out upon the Pacific, which is only about forty-five miles distant.

The country in the foreground is not untypical of the Guatemalan highlands. It is pine-covered, except where the trees have been hacked down. A small farm shows at the lower left, and something of its history can be read from mere observation. Apparently the house was built close to where the crops were originally being grown. These fields eroded away, or else became infertile, and they have now been allowed to go back to brush and saplings. Then fields were cleared farther down the hill and at some distance from the house. Corn is now growing in these fields, planted along the contour lines as a delaying-action against erosion.

At the top of the hill above the house the trees have recently been cut off, and a rough pasture-land is left. Pine saplings are already springing up to restore the forest.

As the opalescent sky would indicate, the picture was taken in early morning, about seven o'clock. The uncertain light also accounts for the mingling of shadows and highlights.

39 Land Use

— Like Mexico and unlike the more southern Central American republics, Guatemala is thickly inhabited or over-inhabited, at least in the highlands. Pressure of population produces such a scene as this, which shows the attempt — so to speak — to eat the cake and have it too, by growing both forest and corn on the same land. It reminds one of southern Italy where the peasants grow wheat beneath their olive trees. The location is near Sumpango, about 25 miles west of Guatemala City.

The hillside is so steep that it probably cannot grow crops for many years without suffering severe erosion. In an effort to prevent this, the corn has been planted in individual hills along furrows contoured to the hillside, as can be seen on the opposite slope. At most, however, corn gives little protection to the land and the best hope lies in the nature of the soil, which is volcanic ash, not only rich, but also well adapted for soaking up even a heavy rain instead of being washed away by it.

The pines themselves offer additional testimony to the pressure of population. Tufts of green are left only at their tops, since the branches have been lopped off for firewood or charcoal. These pines of the southern mountains are of many different varieties, only a few of which grow also in the United States. Most of them are long-needled, like the sapling at the left in the picture. They are also likely to be rapid-growing, but do not attain the great size of our ponderosas and sugar-pines.

 Famous Bridge

✦ Opened for use in 1592, the original bridge over the Esclavos River still bore the highway traffic in 1955, three and a half centuries later. A new bridge is planned about a hundred yards downstream, fortunately offering a view of the old structure.

The bridge consists of massive stone piers linked by heavy brick arches, eleven in all. By its very bulk it acts as a dam, bluntly opposing the rush of the current, and by its very weight and mass seeming to dare the water to do its worst. It offers a contrast to the more lightly built structure over the Laja (see Picture 12) which spans an equally broad stream by means of fewer piers and flatter arches, thus letting the water escape easily beneath. On the upstream side here shown, the piers go out to sharp points, breaking the force of the water, and making it harder for tree-trunks to lodge. Naturally, no structure can stand so long in a tropical climate without damage. The bridge has called for repairs on various occasions, and newer stonework and mortar can be seen in several places. In fact, a little pointing-up would be in order at the present time, and certainly the plants should be removed from the masonry before their roots cause damage.

Though popularly said to bear its name because it was a bridge built by slaves, the truth seems to be that the river bore that name before the bridge did, and that it was so-called in pre-Conquest times, because its banks were the home of certain Indians, who were held as slaves by the rulers of Guatemala. Another legend associated with the bridge is that its building was only accomplished through a league with the devil, a dull and hackneyed version of a wide-spread folk-tale. More interesting is the probability, that the two architects, Francisco Tirado and Diego Felipe, were Indians. (See also page 83.)

The rushing torrent on the river is sufficient demonstration of why a bridge was needed. Without one, land-transportation would have been absolutely blocked for the six months during which the stream could neither be forded nor ferried. Note also the high water mark indicated by the point at which brushwood has been lodged.

The women doing their washing furnish one of the commonest sights of Mexico and Central America. The girls here are comparatively light-colored, and are of the mixed Spanish blood of eastern Guatemala, not the almost pure Indians of the highlands.

Two weeks later, when we returned this way, the stream had risen several feet, and the ground where the laundry is lying was then under water.

41 Road Work

✦ Although machines are generally used for the original construction of highways in Mexico and Central America, maintenance is often a matter of handwork. . . .

In the upper picture the rains have brought a few tons of earth sliding down from a cut and spilling onto the edge of the pavement. With no more mechanical assistance than a primitive ox-cart and a pair of coal-black "bulls," a single workman is shoveling away, and eventually will clear the highway. The scene is about five miles west of Las Cruces in southern Mexico, looking south of west toward the Sierra Madre del Sur, the mountains which Thomas Gage knew as Quelenes (see page 93). The road, though here heading straight at the mountains, turns and swings around the shoulder to the right. The countryside is here thorn-scrub with some grassland, but with a few cleared fields and some houses showing. . . .

The lower picture shows the road a few miles west of Jutiapa in eastern Guatemala. This stretch has been graded to Pan-American standards, probably with the aid of machinery. It is wide, with easy curves, and good ditches. It has never been paved, however, and has received only the roughest kind of stone-and-gravel surfacing. The end of every rainy season, therefore, finds it full of gullies and chuck-holes, with its ditches blocked here and there.

To get it back into some kind of shape, fifteen men are here working. They have no animals to aid them, and their most complicated machine is a wheel-barrow. Large primitive-looking hoes with home-made handles are the chief tools. In the United States the maintenance of such a large pay-roll to accomplish so little moving of dirt would soon bankrupt any road-contractor.

The background shows the undistinguished and infertile country of eastern Guatemala. A few clearings can be seen, but most of the low rolling hills are grown over with scrub.

In the distance a volcano pokes its head above the lower hills. It shows the usual silhouette of a cone cut off at the top, and is probably Suchitan.

At this point the road has begun its descent from the highlands, but has not yet dropped over the edge of the plateau. The altitude is about 4000 feet, with the volcano rising some 3000 feet higher.

 Coffee

● Anyone not knowing the answer would take this for the picture of a tropical jungle. It is, however, a well-cultivated and highly productive coffee-grove, just north of Coatepeque in Salvador. In the foreground the berries may be seen growing thickly on the twigs. Coffee ripens in the winter months, and in the picture (taken in October) the berries are still green.

The glossy-leafed coffee-bushes, about six or eight feet tall, form the solid lower story of vegetation. Above them grow the trees which have been planted as shade for the coffee-bushes. Various species of trees are thus used.

At the right a single banana-stock thrusts its long fronds up through the thick growth of coffee. Plantings of bananas are frequently used to shade the young coffee-bushes, but what this single one is doing here is hard to explain. Bananas and coffee are the great money-crops of Central America, but the large-scale commercial growing of bananas is confined to the lowlands, and no extensive plantings can be seen along the highway.

The altitude here is about 2500 feet. Throughout Central America coffee is cultivated at altitudes from 2000 to 6000 feet. Conditions in this part of Salvador are excellent for coffee, as the luxuriance of this "finca" testifies.

One thing that a coffee-grove certainly is not is photogenic. Even this somewhat confused picture was made possible only by the accident that the highway is at this place just at a proper height to permit a picture across the tops of the bushes. Many tourists, in fact, will drive through miles of coffee-groves without even realizing what they are seeing.

43 "Thus Ends..."

— "Thus ends the rash man," runs the inscription on a monument erected a few miles west of the city of San Salvador. On the pedestal is placed the badly-smashed wreck of an American car, as an object lesson. To add an additional vividness, the car rests upon a seeming roadway of large and very rough stones, thus indicating how disastrous the overturn would be. Similar statues may be found elsewhere in Central America, and with them may also be compared the crosses that stand along the highway, marking spots of fatalities.

In theory, such a gruesome memorial may be considered educational, tending to induce safer driving by threat and fear. The tourist from the United States, however, is more likely to view it as only another evidence of that cult of death which the Latin American seems to cultivate, and which may be considered to reach its height in the bull ring.

Meantime the native Salvadorian at the right looks back curiously at the photographer, as if saying, "Next time try the bull-team." The small boy is unconcerned.

This cart represents the traditional mode of wheeled transportation through Central America, and its driver is not at all likely to become involved in a traffic accident, especially as long as he keeps off the pavement and on a paralleling dirt road.

These paralleling tracks are often of interest. Many of them, as here, are worn down well below the level of the ground, thus showing that they are probably the ancient roads. The drivers of ox-carts prefer them, even when they are deep in mud and puddled with water.

This cart, which might accurately be called a "stake-side," differs from those to be seen in the more primitive parts of the country, especially farther south, in that it has spoked wheels, not solid ones.

In the background the magnificent tropical tree seems to harmonize with the cart; the power-line, with the wrecked car.

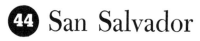 San Salvador

● In Latin America, wealth and luxury and display concentrate in the capital cities. To a degree wholly unknown in the tradition of the United States each capital thus becomes the focus of "society" and "culture."

The scene, on the western outskirts of San Salvador, displays the Plaza de Las Américas which the highway skirts on leaving the city. In the center of the well-kept park, with a lawn and ornamental trees, rises a gigantic monument of Christ, his right hand pointing benignly upward. He stands upon a gigantic replica of the globe; it, in turn, upon a high built stone pedestal, with a great cross facing toward each point of the compass.

Although with their assumption of independence, the Latin-American countries generally cast off all official connection with the church along with their allegiance to Spain, they remain almost wholly Roman Catholic, and such religious manifestations as this are much commoner than in the United States.

Beyond the well-trimmed lawn of the plaza stand the modern residences of wealthy Salvadorians, shadowed by tall ornamental trees and stately palms. Modernism is the prevailing mode in present-day domestic architecture in these countries, though it is often what might almost be called "Victorian modernism," so much is it adorned with gimcracks and unfunctional gadgets.

Beyond the buildings rise the slopes of the volcano San Salvador, its peak reaching to 6398 feet, nearly 4000 above the level of the city. . . .

The lower picture, showing the volcano almost to its peak, has been included as a demonstration of the rapidity with which weather conditions can change in this region. The two photographs were taken only about five minutes apart, a little after eight in the morning. Yet in that brief interval the cloud had almost disappeared from the mountain.

The lower picture also shows someone's cook, starting out from one of the elegant houses, off to market with her basket.

In this picture, also, the clearings on the steep slope of the mountain may be well observed. These extend, in patches, almost to the peak.

Salvadorian Landscape

● With the opening of the highway and the influx of heavy tourist traffic, this is likely to be a much photographed scene, and may end by becoming a pictorial cliché. It can be photographed directly from the side of the highway, and has already appeared in a Salvadorian guidebook, which goes on to describe the view as "the most beautiful panorama in a country famed for its scenery," and to comment that "the valley, intensely cultivated, appears as a polychromatic chessboard, with the volcano as an imposing background." There is no need to quarrel with this ecstatic judgment.

Noteworthy is the adaptation of agriculture to the terrain, as sometimes happens when primitive farmers after long experience seem naturally to work out a good system of land-utilization. (But compare Pictures 25 and 38). The stream-courses descending from the mountain are marked by shadowed gullies, and by winding lines of tree-growth. Between them the fields are laid out, each planted along contour, so that there is even some effect of terracing. The more intensely cultivated lowland fields yield gradually to the rougher clearings of the mountain slopes. These, as in the preceding picture, extend almost to the summit.

This is a region of mixed and rich agriculture — corn, tobacco, indigo, fruit, sugar, and coffee. In the foreground, just at the foot of the hill, we have what is apparently a coffee-plantation. All that can be seen is the leafy cover afforded by the shade trees (compare Picture 42). Some suggestion of the rich volcanic nature of the soil is given by the dark appearance of the cultivated field just to the left of this grove.

This is the Salvadorian plateau, the road here being at an altitude of about 2500 feet. The location is not far from the turn-off to the city of San Vicente. The two-peaked volcano bears that same name, and rises to a height which one of my maps states to be 7131 feet and another to be 7354 feet. Such discrepancies, however, are generally to be expected in the region along the highway, since the delicate work of accurate mapping remains far from complete. The nearer peak of the mountain is about five miles distant by air line. From that peak the Pacific Ocean should be in full view, about twenty miles away.

Although this region is intensively cultivated, and also densely populated, very few houses or other evidences of habitation can be discerned. The people generally live in villages, and not, after the fashion in the United States, on their individual farms, in scattered farm-houses.

The picture was taken about nine in the morning. The little patch of cloud on the mountain may be either a remnant of the night-fog, or a precursor of the rising cumulus clouds that will produce the afternoon thunderstorm.

46 Lempa Crossing

— The Lempa is the largest river of Central America emptying into the Pacific. It rises in Guatemala, flows through Honduras, and then bisects Salvador from north to south. But these are small countries, and the stream's total length is only about two hundred miles. During the rainy season the Lempa might pass as one of the world's great rivers, but during the dry season it shrinks to insignificance.

In the midground of the picture rise the towers of the graceful Cuscatlán Bridge, its overall length of 1350 feet making it the longest span on the highway in Central America. It was wholly financed by Salvador, was built by a United States construction company under the supervision of Salvadorian engineers, and was opened in 1942. On that occasion a memorial postage stamp was issued.

In earlier times a ferry was maintained for the crossing of the river. (See pages 148 and 150.) Thomas Gage records the curious fact that in his time anyone who had committed "any heinous crime or murther," if he managed to escape across this river, could have immunity as long as he lived on its other side.

In the foreground, the seemingly quadrupedal nature of the woman is the result of there being two women, one behind the other, each carrying a basket on her head, in Central-American fashion.

The ox-cart, at the right, with its solid wheels and cloth cover, is wholly traditional, and could serve as the model of the cart represented in Squier's book of 1852.

Beyond the women is a crude outdoor market, of the sort much favored in Salvador. The *Alto* (stop) sign calls upon the motorist to pay his bridge toll.

Beyond the river rises the Volcán Siguatepec (3200 feet), with clearings for fields all the way to its summit. On the lower slopes are older clearings, now reverting to scrub, probably because they have been abandoned as the result of erosion.

From the point of the preceding picture, the highway has descended more than two thousand feet. The bridge is only about a hundred feet above sea level, because of the deep valley which the Lempa has cut across the whole country.

47 Environs of Custom House

— As stated in connection with the pictures of San Salvador, wealth and luxury in Central America concentrate in the capital cities. By contrast, on the Honduran frontier of Salvador, the custom house consists of a dirty old wooden building, looking out on the view here shown. The foraging sow, long-legged and skinny, lacks mud-puddles only because there has been no rain lately. In the midground stand picturesque but unsanitary thatched huts. Cars of tourists crossing the border are merely parked in this open space, completely exposed to tropical sun and downpours. The numerous population of the huts is free to wander over and look on curiously, while the officers go through the suitcases. This picture is printed in the hope that its publication will aid improvement.

Note the old fashioned hand-pump. Since it seems unlikely that sanitary facilities (if any) are kept at a safe distance from this well, any drinking of its water is not recommended. In fact, wells of this sort give point to the wry Central-American toast, "Saludos, amoebas!"

In the background may be seen the line of the highway, and above it a hillside of thorn-scrub. The lower part of the hillside has once been cleared for fields, but has now gone back to brush.

48 Men on the Road—Honduras

• The one with the home-made carrying-yoke we overtook about a mile south of Choluteca. He was happy to stand for the picture, and enjoyed the candy we gave him afterwards. He is carrying a good load, for his bags are full of bottles of milk. What the hot sun is doing to the milk one would rather not consider; it is making the veins stand out on his arm, and has made him unbutton his shirt. He thus displays the undershirt, which he probably wears to escape the "tropical chill."

He is apparently of mixed blood, with a heavy and not very intelligent-looking face. Except for his sandals, he shows no detail of local costume, and is wearing nondescript factory-made clothes — as, indeed, is to be expected, south of Guatemala. Note, however, the inevitable machete — in this case scarcely more than a big knife — which he carries at the back of the yoke, its handle showing against the sky. . . .

The other is José Blas García, a much neater and superior-looking type, though only a landless agricultural worker and unable to read or write. He came along while we were eating lunch by the roadside south of Nacaome. He stopped, obviously as curious about tourists as they might be about him. We talked, and passed him various things to eat, all of which he munched curiously as novelties — but, with a high respect for the utility of food, rejecting nothing. He had never eaten olives before, or — I imagine — crackers. He did not even know the Spanish word for olive.

Afterwards, he willingly posed, displaying his machete as requested. He is a neater-looking figure than the milkman, though not really better-dressed, except for his newer hat. In fact, he lacks footwear, displaying the wide-spread and well-developed toes of a man who habitually walks barefoot. He, also, shows his undershirt. His only baggage is the little bundle lying behind him, though he is on his way from Nacoame to Choluteca, job-hunting.

He had hardly started the journey and had 25 miles to go; it was already one o'clock, but he seemed in no hurry. Either he was living up to the ideals of the land of *mañana,* or he hoped to pick up a ride in a truck.

Like the other, he is of mixed blood, though some shades lighter in complexion. His face is a fine one, suggesting both a strong character and intelligence. His conversation also indicated intelligence, and we left him with the feeling the Hondurans must be of good stock, if he could be taken as a type.

 **49** "Dogs and Vultures"

✚ The title, echoing no less a classical source than the opening lines of the *Iliad,* gives some indication of what the reality must have been at the Achaean beachhead, after Chryses had incited Apollo's vengeance against the captors of his daughter. Fortunately, the body here is not that of some warrior slain by a shaft of the God of the Silver Bow, but only of a small pig, perhaps killed by a truck on the road.

The three dogs held possession of the corpse, though by the time we arrived on the scene they were almost glutted to satiety. This is a feast such as they seldom experience, for in Central America most of the dogs are no better than Asiatic pariahs. The one still eating shows every rib.

Gathered to the feast that will eventually be theirs is a company of of some scores of buzzards. By a concentrated effort they could easily have driven the cowardly dogs away, but buzzards are not fighters. Drawn as by a magnet, they kept approaching close to the spoil from all directions, gathering like a black cloud. Then, at a snarl of the dogs, the air was suddenly full of buzzards, who flew off to settle down again in a ring.

This is the lowland of Honduras, about five miles north of Choluteca and about that also from tidewater on the Gulf of Fonseca. The soil is poor, and the country is not highly cultivated or thickly inhabited. Even the growth of scrub seems thin. The road is primitive, though "all-weather," and not too rough.

Note the diminutive telephone pole, just on the other side of the road.

50 Honduran Transportation

● Along the highway nothing offers more variety and more interest to the tourist than the varying means of "native" transportation. For reasons which I cannot explain the region around Choluteca in Honduras seems to have developed its own special methods. . . .

The goat-cart, for all I know, may be the only one in Central America. At least, I have never talked to anyone who has seen another one. It is constructed on the model of an ox-cart with solid wheels and "stake sides." The miniature yoke is lashed to the horns of the goats, just as the larger yoke is lashed to the horns of the oxen. Yet it is not a toy, as the load (lying just back of the cart) fully indicates. Probably all this outfit means is that the owner, being too poor to afford oxen, made use of the animals he had.

As his smile shows, he is very proud of his ingenuity. Both he and his wife are wearing a kind of combination of store-clothes and native costume. The side-road in the background shows what was to be expected before the graveling of the highway. . . .

In the lower picture an ox-cart follows two of the handcarts characteristic of this region, and not appearing, to my knowledge, elsewhere in Central America. These, also, are constructed on the model of the ox-cart. By means of one of them even the boy in foreground can transport a load of firewood which must amount to more than three hundred pounds, several times what he could carry on his back. With a little down-grade, as here, the going is easy, but on the level it is hard, and with even a slight up-grade the boy would have to have help at handling the cart. On the whole, it is such hard work that the boy has taken his shirt off and thrown it on the load. He is barefoot, which does not make his work easier. His plainly-showing ribs indicate that he is underweight, but he looks happy enough. After all, he is having his picture taken, and that makes most Central Americans happy, until they learn that they should get money for posing. We passed out some candy after the pictures, and that made everyone even happier.

Note the thin dog trotting behind the first cart, and in the background the usual bushes of thorn-scrub. The highway itself is here well graded but rough.

 Choluteca Valley

— Next to the Lempa, the Choluteca is the largest of the rivers on the Pacific side of Central America. Like the Lempa, it has carved out a broad and deep valley, cut down almost to sea-level. The valley here shows in the distance to the right, largely overgrown with scrub forest, but with some cleared fields. Beyond, the mountains rise to peaks of about 4000 feet, extending off northward toward Salvador.

The location is here about 2000 feet above the level of the valley. The difficult climb which the highway is making, twisting and doubling back on itself, is graphic evidence of the bad effect upon the location of the road which must be attributed to local pressures and to political influences. If the highway, as originally planned, had kept right on to the south from the Choluteca bridge, it would not only have followed the traditional route but would also have crossed level country and been fifty miles shorter. For extraneous reasons, however, it was here forced to turn aside to a longer route, across rough country, and over a summit of more than 4000 feet. (See page 28.) The only good excuse for this re-routing is that the highway would thus open up new country. But, as the picture demonstrates, much of this country is hilly and rough, and not capable of great development.

The road itself is well graded and not excessively step, though very twisty. Little traffic passes over this section, and the solitary jeep in the distance is somewhat remarkable.

Close at hand the slopes are mostly covered with scrub-growth, though a pine tree shows on the skyline at the left. Some clearings can be seen, and a steeply sloping field at the left is planted in corn. Lower down on the left is a small planting of bananas, and other banana stocks show on the hillside, scattered here and there. In this region, however, the soil is comparatively poor — not the rich volcanic ash of the Guatemalan highlands and the Salvadorian plateau.

Though the clouds are largely stratus and do not look very threatening, the blackness of some of them indicates rain, and a storm broke over the mountains only a few minutes after the picture was taken.

52 Men on the Road—Nicaragua

● The man in white is only on the road in Nicaragua by the grace of the twenty feet separating him from the decrepit fence and gate. He is a border-guard, complete with military cap and side-arm. He has walked up from the custom house, to open the gate and let us through into Honduras. In the meantime, he is happy to stand for a picture, striking a pose to indicate that he is at once informal and alertly military, even if he fails to have much of a uniform. As is common in Nicaragua, he is very dark, and is chiefly of Indian blood.

In Central America, a region of small countries, the traveler becomes uncomfortably aware of this smallness because of the many boundaries that he has to cross. At the top of the hill stands another custom-house, where the north-bound motorist must again pass through the same tedious inspection for immigration and customs that he has just finished. Within two hours he will have to stop once more at the Choluteca inspection-post. And before the end of the day he will be forced to pass the double-double inspection to let him leave Honduras and enter Salvador. . . .

Below, two wayfarers near Lake Nicaragua stand for portraits, but not before the crafty looking one on the right has extracted some money from the photographer. (Such requests are rare to the south of Guatemala.)

The big fellow stands solidly and stolidly, holding his ox-goad. Like the border-guard, he is dark, and he seems to have a share of Negro blood, as would be expected in the lowlands. The little man, the leader of the pair, is quick, interested, and somewhat lighter in complexion. He stands staring at the camera, displaying the ever-present machete.

They both wear nondescript clothing, having no need for coats in this always-tropical region. The only unusual feature is that they are well booted, perhaps because they have to work in forested country.

The background shows the thickly wooded country along the lakeshore. (See Picture 58.) A thatched hut stands in the shelter of the trees, and along the road lie three big partly squared logs, cut from some great tropical tree of the near-by forest. . . .

In the upper picture the road has been graded to Pan-American standards and graveled. In the lower picture it is graveled, but has not yet been graded to standard, and the timbers have been thrown down carelessly into its ditch.

53 Backwoods Country

— Among connoisseurs of backwoods, those of Nicaragua hold a very high rating. Here we see an interesting transition stage. A few years ago there would have been no communication-line through this country, except a primitive road — or nothing but a horse-trail. Subsistence farming would have been the only possible way of living. Even yet, in this country a few miles south of Somoto, much impression of the old-time isolation still remains. A woman and a boy, driving a heifer, walk barefoot along the road. Farther off, a cow holds possession.

At the left a poor little corn-patch occupies a bit of level ground at the base of the hill. Beyond it, across an abandoned field, is a small plantation of bananas. In the old days, such produce had to be consumed close to where it was grown. There was no chance of a profitable money-crop, because transportation charges by ox-cart or pack-train are estimated at approximately fifty cents (U. S.) per ton-mile. Once trucks can penetrate a country, transportation charges drop to perhaps one tenth of what they have been.

At the right of the road, in the distance, are some better-cultivated fields, and possibly some produce may already have started to go to market from this region. Large areas of Nicaragua still remain undeveloped because of lack of communications, and there is much chance for the expansion of population. Once a highway has been put through, coffee and other money-crops can be grown.

The road here is in itself of considerable interest. It has not yet been paved, but has a hard surface, and has been laid out and graded to Pan-American standards. A broad right of way has been retained, as indicated by the distance between the fences — in themselves, poor as they are, a mark of the new era, since they must have been erected since the laying-out of the highway. A road such as this, even though unpaved, is in most ways more pleasant to drive than the antiquated narrow and twisty asphalt which is standard paved highway in Central America.

Another symbol of the opening era is the small structure in the distance. It is a new school, one of the many now being built in Central America. Like most of the contemporary buildings of the region, whether domestic or otherwise, it is modernistic in design.

Beyond the school, in the background, rise the scrub-covered hills, here and there cleared for fields or little plantations of bananas. The altitude of these ridges is close to 3000 feet, high enough for pines, and one or two of these, having escaped ax and fire, still rise against the skyline.

54 One-House Village

• When we halted by the road-side to change drivers a few miles north of Estelí, we had no concern about stopping close to a primitive-looking house, such as one often passes in the Nicaraguan backwoods. Suddenly we were aware that people enough for a whole village were pouring out and bearing down on us in friendly curiosity. I quickly brought the camera to bear. They continued out to the road, and I lined them up there and took more pictures, and then passed out the candy — though much to the depletion of the candy-bag, as the size of the crowd would make certain. We had a very jolly time.

Though I am no anthropologist, I tried to determine what might be called the social structure of the group. The oldish-looking woman, seen at the center, was the matriarch, and apparently the grandmother, though she was probably under fifty. She definitely ran the show. She saw to it that the children and younger women stood in their places for the picture. There were three mothers, who are to be distinguished by their slightly larger size or by the babies they are carrying. There were thirteen children, including babies in arms. All of these can be counted in the picture, if you look sharply for figures half-concealed behind bushes. No men were in evidence, and I presume that they were off working, though I did not ask any embarrassing questions. A considerable range of complexion is to be noted in the offspring.

The costume offers nothing of much interest, consisting either of store-clothes or of clothes made up from the cheapest possible material to be bought in stores. Everyone is barefoot. This need not be counted a hardship, but it means the risk of parasitical infections, especially since the house undoubtedly lacks sanitary facilities.

It is worth noting that the little boy in the foreground is naked only from the waist up, and that the others are fully clothed. In the tropical lowlands the boys commonly go naked until they are half-grown. (I sometimes wonder if they then don't put on pants and a machete at the same time, since the two seem to go together like a horse and carriage.)

Apparently these people all live in the same house, and would seem, from their smiles and interest in life, to live there happily. The residence itself deserves some attention, being a rather poor and ordinary tropical thatched hut, which has sprouted some lean-tos for the accommodation of this matriarchal clan. It has nothing but stakes for its side-walls, through which the wind can blow, though the altitude is here 3000 feet, and the weather can sometimes be chilly. This suggests what I have often found some cause to think, that the Nicaraguans are a lowland people, who have never quite adjusted themselves to having migrated to the colder climate of the mountains, and continue to build houses that are essentially those of the low country.

The region here is stony and infertile. Note the pile of rocks at the left, just behind the woman with the laundry on her head.

The tree — they called it a jicarilla — indicates by its size and by its height before the spread of the branches begins, that it originally grew in a forest that has more recently been cleared off by man.

 **55** Estelí

● Though it is a provincial capital (population about 6000) the average tourist might be likely to describe Estelí in the words applied by a nineteenth-century traveler to another Nicaraguan town, "distinguished as being utterly destitute of a single object of interest," Or he might, at most, be pleased that the owner of the gas-station was "up-and-coming" enough to accept a traveler's check without question.

But, as here seen, it is really an "unspoiled" town, not yet made over for the benefit of tourists — crude though it may be, still rewarding as an object of study.

Consider, for instance, that this displays itself a region of "horse culture," even though the animals are small and scrawny. The trappings show a combination of elaboration and poverty. The saddle "cloths" are of leather, some of them handworked, unusually large — perhaps to keep insects off. The elaborate tassels on the rump of the farther animal probably serve the same purpose, although also for ornament. (This "horse," indeed, is a mule.) In another picture note the extremely primitive nature of the saddle — a saddle-cloth with some wadded up material to serve as horn and cantle. . . .

There is also more else to note than space allows. In the top picture the construction of the houses shows itself clearly to be mud or adobe supported by a wooden frame — very solid, and much better adapted to cold weather than the hut shown in the preceding picture. As usual in backwoods countries, there is what might be called lavish use of wood, though the roofs are of tile. . . .

The bottom picture shows an outdoor market, chiefly dealing in fruit and vegetables. The town may not have a paved street, but it has a curb and gutter. Also, the bicycle is entering into competition with the horse. The little girl and her mother who are buying fruit give the suggestion of belonging to the town's upper crust, by the better-looking clothes they are wearing. On the whole, however, the clothing does not indicate extreme poverty. People are wearing store-clothes, and most of them have shoes. The young laundress seems well-enough fed and clothed.

These three scenes, all taken along the highway, should not be taken as a full portrait of the town. There are better buildings than these, but the traveler naturally turns toward the more picturesque and typical.

 Wet Road

— At Tipitapa, the outlet of Lake Managua passes across the Pan-American Highway. Most of the year no water flows out at all, but after heavy rains it can look like this. Actually, there is a bridge that can be taken by following a detour off to the right, but no maps or guidebooks seem to offer this information. We learned in what might well have turned out to be the hard way.

We came around the curve on the other side, saw a truck wallowing across ahead of us, and hesitated. An accommodating gentleman waved encouragement from this end, and we decided to try. The water came up about to the floor of the car, and the driver had difficulty in keeping on the road. There was danger of running off to one side into deeper water, but the helper on this end kept motioning back and forth. So we made it through.

When we went north, at the time this picture was taken, the water was still higher, and we detoured around by the bridge. The water is not actually as deep as it looks. The boy at the right, who is up to his hips in water, is either sitting down, or off the edge of the pavement. The little fellow just starting to wade in with his mother, will get through without doing anything more than just submerging his bare buttocks.

Lake Managua itself, is only about a mile to the left of this crossing. Squier, visiting the region in 1849, described the mud flats around the outlet as "the dwelling place of numerous alligators." These days, however, such creatures live a hunted life, and probably none are left of large-enough size to endanger the child here making the crossing. In earlier times they were held in considerable fear.

The two pole-lines show the contrast of up-to-date and primitive, so often to be observed in Central America. The one is of steel, generally favored in the tropics as not being subject to the attack of termites. The wooden pole-line is constructed from native trees, which rarely grow straight. In fact, the poles along the highway offer continual variety and can often be a source of amusement to the tourist. The ones here seen are much less fantastic in shape than many elsewhere.

The open landscape in the distance is typical of this part of Nicaragua, where the land has been cleared for fields or for cattle-pasture, with some large trees left standing for shade.

The picturesque name Tipitapa is believed to be derived from the combination of local Indian words *tetl-petlatl-pan*. This has been shortened and simplified for pronunciation in Spanish, chiefly by dropping the non-Spanish sound indicated by -tl- or reducing it to -t-. The meaning is literally "stone-mat-place," and the reference is to a flat-topped rock-formation near-by.

57 Tropical Landscape—I

● The variety of landscape afforded by the tropics can be a continual source of wonder to anyone driving the highway. Here, about twelve miles south of Rivas, close to Lake Nicaragua but looking away from it, the traveler sees a landscape of an open park-like aspect. With its rich grass and its cattle peacefully grazing on a knoll, it might be taken for a countryside in the eastern United States, or almost in England.

Such a landscape, here as in most other countries, is largely the result of man's handiwork. The underbrush and most of the trees have been cleared away, and those that remain have been left for shade, or as a reserve of timber to be harvested later, or merely because they were so big that they required too much work for removal. The clean boles rising to a considerable height without side-branches indicate that they originally grew in a thick forest. The trees themselves, by their unusual forms of growth and by their buttress-roots, indicate that they are not the oaks or elms of more northern regions, but are thoroughly of the tropics.

The foreground shows a crudely built barbed-wire fence; this side of it, the muddy tracks along the highway show where the ox-carts pass back and forth.

This section of Nicaragua is notable for its trees. Stephens, traveling in 1840, left a description of this region which could actually be used for this picture: "The fields were covered with high grass, studded with noble trees. . . . Herds of cattle gave it a home-like appearance." The term *savanna* is often applied to such a landscape.

This picture may be profitably contrasted with the next one, which was taken only about three miles farther down the road.

58 Tropical Landscape—II

● About fifteen miles south of Rivas and five from the Costa Rican border, the tourist encounters country which will come closer to his probable idea of the deep tropics than any other along the highway. The road here runs close to the shore of Lake Nicaragua, which can often be seen, as in this picture, through the break in the trees near the center. Being so close to the lake, this region is not much affected by the dry season, and so the vegetation assumes the luxuriance associated with the forests of the Amazon. Great tropical trees, of many different species, here rear their heads skyward, and long rope-like lianas trail earthward from them. This thoroughly tropical scene offers a fine contrast to that of the preceding picture, which suggests the temperate zone, although the two spots are only three miles apart.

In the midst of this jungle the people have cleared a little space, and erected two huts. These are well thatched, with steeply sloping roofs and heavy overhangs, to shed the torrential rains. But they might be described as shelters rather than houses, since they are almost wholly open at the sides, with no real walls at all. Protection against the cold is not needed in this region, which is only eleven degrees from the equator and about one hundred feet above sea-level. The hut at the left has a shelter built out from it, which would give protection from sun, if not from rain.

Since there are no fields near these huts, the people may be fishermen, or laborers on the near-by ranches. Some lumbering is done in these forests, but the extent of the woodland is not great enough to provide much employment. (See Picture 52.) In such lush tropical surroundings living is likely to come easily, and high infant-mortality keeps the population within the limits of the food-supply. Because of the ease of living in Nicaragua, the early Spaniards called it "Mahomet's Paradise."

Whether this paradise had its quota of houris, is not stated. The two little girls who ran up to get into the picture seem scarcely to qualify. The one on the left has some mingling of Negro blood, as is to be expected in the coastal regions. Though both are barefooted, the one on the left is remarkably well clothed, in a factory-made dress with even a touch of styling about it. Her hair is also very neatly dressed. The population of these huts must be considerable. No less than four adults may be made out in the background, all looking curiously at the photographer.

Some commentators upon Nicaragua would suggest that the lighter complexion of the smaller girl may have some linkage with the occupation of this country by our marines during the nineteen-twenties, but she would have to be a granddaughter.

59 Ocean Glimpse

• Although the highway, throughout most of its course, lies within the drainage basin of the Pacific Ocean, glances at any open water are rare. Here, a few miles south of La Cruz, in northern Costa Rica, the view is a little north of west, toward the Salinas Bay, and the open ocean beyond. Punta Zacate (Grassy Point) lies at the left. Across the bay, beyond the small rock-like island, the view extends into Nicaragua. The landscape, with its thick but low forest and the occasional clearings is typical of the province of Guanacaste, through which the road runs for many miles in northwestern Costa Rica. Coarse bunch-grass grows on the slope in the foreground, which has undoubtedly been artificially cleared.

This spot, as it happens, represents a geographical curiosity. Although from the point of taking a picture the distance to the nearest shore of the bay is only about three miles, the slope in the foreground represents the continental divide. From its top, only a short distance to the right, the water flows the other way and reaches the Caribbean Sea. Probably nowhere else is the divide so close to either ocean. Water falling here on the Atlantic side of the watershed will have to flow a distance of approximately two hundred miles through the Sapoa River, Lake Nicaragua and the San Juan River, before reaching the Caribbean.

This spot, with its beautiful view and its likelihood of ocean breezes, would be an excellent one for the location of some motel or other accommodation for tourists. Also, the bay undoubtedly offers good possibilities for fishing.

🔟 Ox-Carts

● The ox-cart has been the chief means of heavy transport in the leveler parts of Central America since the establishment of Spanish folkways. It has apparently changed little in design throughout centuries. The introduction of iron axles and of axle-grease has increased its efficiency, and silenced the screeching of the wheels which used to herald its advance.

In the upper picture we see a fine team of dun-colored "bulls" against a background of thick jungle-forest in the lowlands of Guanacaste. The cartwheels are solid. The body is "stake side," with boards placed inside the stakes to hold the load of corn and oranges. This is well covered with a tarpaulin against rain. A Costa Rican flag is displayed on the side, probably because this is near the Nicaraguan border, and there had been a "border incident" shortly before this time. The teamster, here in the Costa Rican lowlands, may show a little admixture of non-Spanish blood. In his left hand he holds the long, traditional ox-goad; in his right hand, the ever-present machete. . . .

The lower picture was taken at the village of El Tejar in the Central Meseta of Costa Rica — that rich-soiled highland region of little valleys and undulating hills, cupped among higher mountains, where the chief cities of the republic and most of its population are to be found. El Tejar is at the edge of this area, a few miles south of the ancient city of Cartago, just where the highway enters the Talamanca Mountains.

This driver is thoroughly European in type, as is to be expected in the Meseta. Neither in physiognomy, nor, indeed, in costume, would he create any comment in a rural district of the United States. Only his ox-goad — and, of course, his machete — would seem unusual.

He is carting dirt from an excavation being made along the road. His oxen are younger and smaller than those in the other picture. The manner of lashing the yoke to the horns can be seen clearly.

The cart is elaborately painted in geometrical designs. Carts thus ornamented are usual in this part of Costa Rica and toy-size replicas are the principal souvenirs offered for sale to tourists. I have been unable to discover whether these decorated carts have any connection with the even more elaborately painted ones of Sicily. Any direct linkage seems the more unlikely in that the Sicilian carts generally bear representational paintings.

In the background, as in the next picture, may be seen the extensive use of corrugated iron for buildings. As is usual in Costa Rican towns the architecture shows little that is distinctive.

61 Angel

— The Central American countries are highly religious, none more so than Costa Rica. Not infrequently the tourist encounters some procession on the highway.

On this Sunday morning, October 9, the town of Grecia was celebrating the festival of the Virgin of Socorro. As part of the ceremonies a number of little girls are dressed as angels, adorned with flowers, placed on litters, and carried on the shoulders of the men. Here we see one of them returning from church. With her straight hair and broad face she seems rather too heavy and unethereal to be a good member of the heavenly host. (But perhaps there is a need for buxom angels.)

The contrast of Costa Rica with all the other countries of Central America here comes out strikingly. The men are tall, Spanish in type, with no suggestion of Indian blood. In fact, throughout the highlands of Costa Rica, Indian ancestry is no more to be expected than it is in most parts of the United States. The two interested and well-dressed children in the lower right could appear in any of our towns, even though the little boy is barefoot.

The dress and general appearance of the people also indicate the individuality of the country. The extremes of wealth and poverty are not common there, and the typical citizen is a small farmer or a small tradesman of a town. As compared with the colorful inhabitants of the other countries, the Costa Ricans seem well-fed and contented, but perhaps a little dull. For the attraction of tourists the country must depend upon its beauiful scenery.

The appearance of the town is equally Costa Rican. The extensive use of corrugated iron suggests some not very up-and-coming part of the United States, rather than any other country of Central America. The gigantic palm tree, whose fronds breaks the skyline, is the only obvious tropical touch, and this might be found in Florida or California.

The church looks much more like the First Methodist in some midwestern town than it does like the baroque edifices of Mexico or Guatemala. It is built of wood over a steel frame — genuine imitation Gothic. It is, however, fairly typical of the ecclesiastical architecture of Costa Rica.

Grecia is the equivalent of Greece in Spanish, and this identity of names has given rise to a local legend about the church. As some of the local inhabitants maintain, the structural steel was really supposed to be shipped to Grecia, the country, but by confusion ended up at Grecia, the town!

62 Waiting for the Bus—Cold Country

✛ Once a highway is put through, anywhere in Central America, the bus becomes the chief means of communication. The traditional ox-drawn transportation is too expensive for the long haul, and there are few trucks and almost no private cars. So the bus must, and does, transport everything short of the larger livestock and the wholesale production of the fields.

Here, almost ten thousand feet up on the Talamanca Mountains, between Cartago and San Isidro, what must be a large proportion of the whole population of the region — fifteen men and boys, a woman, and a baby — are waiting. Some, indeed, are not planning to go, since they will have to take the horses home — these full-grown ones being beyond the ordinary capa-

city of even a Costa Rican bus. In addition, the bus will have to accommodate a good deal of assorted hand-luggage, plus a dozen large sacks of corn
or other produce.

The people are of the ordinary Costa Rican type in personal appearance
and clothing. One of them is wearing a checked sport-shirt, such as might
be seen anywhere in the United States. The number of broad-brimmed
hats is perhaps the only feature that seems Latin-American. These hardy
mountaineers are very lightly clothed, even though the day is rainy and far
from warm at this altitude. In fact, as the clouds suggest, a very heavy
shower has just passed over.

Temperamentally, when facing the camera, these people show the same
variation that is to be expected in a group anywhere. A tall man poses consciously and happily, with arms akimbo. Another one clasps his hands ner-
vously, and looks away from the camera in embarrassment. The others
range between these extremes, some standing stolidly and others with calculated informality.

In keeping with the greater prosperity of Costa Rica, the horses have
regular saddles, not the makeshift affairs which are to be seen in Honduras
(see Picture 55).

These mountains were originally covered with a magnificent forest of
great cypress trees. A few of these are still standing, as in the background of
this picture. Unfortunately, the building of the highway has resulted in
rapid deforestation, and at the right of the picture nothing is left of the
forest except some stumps and a few dead trees, not worth the cutting. A
policy of preserving the trees within a hundred yards of the new road would
not have made much difference in the total amount of timber cut, but would
have rendered the road much more attractive for tourist travel.

63 End—1955

✚ At the southern edge of the town of San Isidro in southern Costa Rica the road sinks back into the primitive. Here, for the last few hundred yards, automobiles rarely penetrate, and the ox-carts no longer follow along the side of the highway, but boldly take to the middle of the road.

During the war a little work was done to the south of this point, and jeeps can still go about ten miles farther. The extension of the road is, however, to be expected soon, and it will reach clear to Panama — with luck, in a few years.

In the picture the first actual break in the roadway can be seen. A fill has been made into the ravine from this end and from the other, but no bridge has been thrown across to connect the two fills, and a sharp gap remains. The present road — or trail, rather — swings to the left just beyond the last small house, and after descending to the stream and fording it, ascends on the other side of the ravine, where its line can be seen among the trees. This trail is chiefly used by pack-trains of horses, and two horses appear faintly, among the trees, just to the right of where the line of the road starts going up to the slight gap in the hills.

Beyond this point an estimated distance of 130 miles separates (1955) the traveler from the road-head extending to the Panama border from the south. Across this stretch, as far as automobiles are concerned, a guidebook properly labels the road as "non-existent." Though it crosses no high mountains, the country is cut by many ravines and is covered with a thick growth of tropical forest, as the picture indicates. Here, indeed, the forest has been considerably affected by man's work, and the hillside at the left has at one time been a cleared field, and is only now returning to forest. The line of demarcation stands out clearly between its younger trees and the older and taller ones near the top of the hill.

At this point — or at least from the end of the jeep-road a few miles south — overland travel thus reverts approximately to the condition of 1601, after Gonzalo Vásquez de Coronado had opened up his mule-trail from Cartago to Panama.

Looking Both Ways

LOOKING BOTH WAYS

Having traveled to the ends of the road, and then returned to his own country, the traveler now looks both ways, and permits himself the luxury of a few reflections. . . .

Our great north-south road is unique. Nowhere else, now or at any other time, have geographical and political barriers been so overcome as to let the private individual, controlling his own means of transportation, travel so far — in safety and ease. While I may perhaps call myself a pioneer, I cannot say that I anywhere on the journey endured hardship, or was subjected to any danger, other than that always accompanying the use of the automobile. As anyone else can do, I traveled in an ordinary car without special equipment. Only on one occasion was I forced to spend the night in lodgings which lacked that symbol of modern civilization known as "modern plumbing." Only about half a dozen times did I lack that other symbol of even greater luxury, "the private bath."

Under such circumstances of comfort I traveled a distance which by great circle must be reckoned as better than one fifth of the earth's circumference. By minimal highway mileage the distance totals about one third of that same unit.

To make comparisons elsewhere on the earth's surface, this is the equivalent of driving from the Bering Strait in Siberia to the southern-most tip of India. Europe is not even large enough to admit the comparison. We must draw in another continent, and then say that the drive in North America is similar to that from northern Finland to the center of French Equatorial Africa.

Just what one sees on this drive — the road, the country along it, and people — the pictures and text should already have demonstrated. I now offer only two comments which may be the more pertinent here, after the reader has vicariously made the journey.

The greatest contrast of the continent lies between the country to the north of the Rio Grande and that to the south of it — between English-speaking and Spanish-speaking America. Though language is the most obvious symbol of this difference, the distinction goes much deeper. To the north, we have the tradition of northwestern Europe, modified by a vigorous new civilization developed in a rich and essentially virgin land. To the south, we have the tradition of a Mediterranean civilization — Iberian, Roman, and Arab — imposed upon regions already thickly inhabited by Indian nations possessing a well-established culture of their own.

The second great contrast is that between civilized and primitive country, or between thickly inhabited and largely uninhabited country. The pictures have been selected with an idea to giving a balanced representation of the whole continent, and it will be noticed how many of them show vacant landscape. Not only does nearly all of the northern road pass through empty spaces, but also almost as wholly lacking in people are the deserts of northern Mexico and even much of the mountain and jungle country farther south. Man in his millions concentrates himself in small patches.

The historical sections have attempted to present the past; the pictures, the present. Some final words may be granted to the future.

Undoubtedly the conditions of travel will steadily, or even rapidly, year by year, improve — unless some blight falls upon our civilization. The road surface will be bettered; the curves, eased; the shoulders, widened. Modern plumbing and the private bath will become universal, instead of nearly so. In addition, the road will be extended — perhaps, to the north; certainly, to the south. Between the time of my own journey and the publication of this book, progress has been made. The extension of the highway to Panama will probably not be delayed for more than a few years. Eventually there will be a linking up with the highway system of South America, but that consummation is still too far in the future to be definitely predicted.

If we accept the premises of civilization, everything that has just been stated may be considered optimistic. But even if we agree that the opening up of a new country by means of a highway, and the extension along it of the modern motel, is to be desired, still the optimism of the preceding paragraph must be a little offset in this one. . . . The highway, it must be admitted, is to some extent a destructive agent. To the north, it brings fire, and there is a danger that five years hence the tourist will drive to Alaska between almost unbroken "picket fences" of burned spruce trees. Everywhere, north and south, the highway opens up the country to ruthless exploitation, by the very fact that it opens the country up at all. Far to the south, the Talamanca Mountains have been stripped of their magnificent forests of cypress, and left skinned and ugly, in the few years since the completion of the highway. Already wild life has almost disappeared along the line of the southern road. Already a few billboards begin to appear.

Such misfortunes and many others are, certainly, inevitable. The highway must serve economic needs other than merely the attraction of the tourist dollar. But we should exercise some foresight, lest the country along the highway should be degraded into a kind of continental slum.

This is not to say that nothing is being done already. There are plenty of signs urging the tourist to be careful with fire, and there are even some rudimentary preparations for fire fighting. The law against shooting along the Alaska Highway is a good one. Mexico has established some national parks.

All these are moves in the right direction. But much more should be done while there is still time. For instance, game-refuges should be established at chosen points along the highway, both north and south. Again, some arrangement, involving compensation to owners, should be made to prevent the deforestation of the immediate strip — say, within a hundred yards — along the highway. The problems that the highway creates need not be accepted as unsolvable.

As to the farther future, no one can write with confidence any more than anyone can confidently predict any other phase of future. As of the present, the highway exists. It is in a transition stage, and will so continue for some time. It is an interesting road to drive — perhaps more interesting now than it will be in a few years, when it has become easier to drive and therefore more driven. By its pictures and text this book has attempted to show that present highway, north and south.

AUTHOR'S NOTE

This book could not have been prepared without the cooperation of many organizations and individuals. To them all, some of whom may at this date have even been lost from my records and have lapsed in my memory — and mine, in theirs — I offer my thanks.

I must mention: the U.S. Bureau of Public Roads; the Office of the Chief of Engineers, U.S. Army; the Esso Touring Service; the International Road Federation; the Dirección General de Turismo (Guatemala).

I am particularly indebted to the officials of the BPR in Central America, of whom I wish especially to mention Thomas A. Jones, of Guatemala City, M. L. Harshberger of San José, and the ever hospitable Springers, of Somoto in Nicaragua.

Along the southern road, I thank, as informants and correspondents, Sr. and Sra. Luis Poyo-Skillen (Mexico City), Sr. Gutierre Tibón (Mexico City), Sr. Alejandro Topete del Valle (Aguascalientes), Mr. and Mrs. H. L. Davis (Oaxaca), Dr. Franz Blom (San Cristóbal), Sr. and Sra. Gustavo Stahl (Guatemala City).

My mentor also for U.S. 40, Mr. E. W. James has been of constant aid in the present project, supplying both advice and materials. In particular, he generously allowed me full use of his extensive manuscript dealing with the history of the southern highway down to 1940.

Most of the works used and quoted in the text are sufficiently well identified there, but I add a few references for books used but not clearly identified.

For the background of the southern highway I am particularly indebted to E. W. James's manuscript (V.S.); valuable for northern Mexico, is P. W. Powell, *Soldiers, Indians, and Silver*. The letters of Cobo form an appendix to the 1944 edition (Mexico, D. F.) of Antonio Vázquez de Espinosa, *Descrip. de la Nueva España*. As official documents may be mentioned

Proposed Inter-American Highway (Doc. #224, 73rd Cong., 2nd Sess.),
Inter-American Highway (Rep. #440, Sen. Rep., 80th Cong. 1st Sess.).
For the New Mexican caravans, see F. V. Scholes's articles in the *New
Mexico Hist. Rev.*, Jan.-Apr.-Oct., 1930. Useful logbooks are *Mexico by
Motor* (American Automobile Association), and Norman D. Ford, *Fiesta
Lands.*

The country along the southern road is much less adequately mapped
than that along the northern. I used the World Aeronautical Charts, but
these are far from being wholly satisfactory. The route maps published
by the American Automobile Association for Mexico, and the Esso maps
for the different countries of Central America are highly useful.

Partly because no authoritative maps are available, and partly because
Latin-American nomenclature is somewhat confused, I have found the
recording of place names to be difficult. I have in general adopted the
spellings and names that appear on the A.A.A. and Esso road maps, since
these are the ones which the tourist will be most likely to use. I have
omitted the accent marks from a few names (e.g., Mexico, Panama) which
may be considered to be Anglicized.